Concepts of Nature and God

Resources for College and University Teaching

Concepts of Nature and God

Resources for College and University Teaching

Philosophy Curriculum Workshop Papers developed at the 1987 NEH Summer Institute on Concepts of Nature and God

Edited by Frederick Ferré

At the Department of Philosophy
The University of Georgia
Athens, Georgia

Printed in the United States of America
Library of Congress Catalogue Card Number: 89-80142

ISBN 0-925615-00-5 (paper, perfect binding)
ISBN 0-925615-01-3 (paper, spiral binding)

The Summer Institute on Concepts of Nature and God was made possible by funding from the National Endowment for the Humanities under Grant Number EH-20633-86. The Director was Frederick Ferré.

Design by Frederick Ferré, using Xerox Ventura Publisher with a Zenith 248 computer and a Hewlett Packard LaserJet Series II printer.

Department of Philosophy
The University of Georgia
Athens, Georgia 30602, U.S.A.

Table of Contents

Workshop on Contemporary Thought

Preface

This book is the product of many people. In the first place it represents the efforts of the twenty-six participants of the summer institute for college and university faculty held on the campus of the University of Georgia, June 15 to July 24, 1987. Those participants came together from sixteen states located in all regions of the United States and included one participant without NEH stipend from West Germany. Most of the participants came from departments of philosophy or religion; one came from a department of chemistry. Whatever the departmental affiliation, all had demonstrated lively interest in the sciences and their humanistic relevance. Most had significant training in one or more of the sciences, and most were experienced in teaching college-level courses at the junction between science and religious or metaphysical world views. Most came from four-year, liberal arts colleges; some came from universities with graduate programs. All twenty-six participants contributed to this book. More details about them can be found in the "Introducing the Participants & Faculty" section at the end.

What drew these people together was a common interest in exploring the point of interaction between changing concepts of nature and of God in the western tradition. The hypothesis of the institute was that there is an important two-way influence between general theories of nature and an epoch's conception of the deity. The task of the institute was to investigate the hypothesis with both historical and systematic methods.

Our program was demanding. Four mornings each week (every weekday except Wednesday) all faculty and participants met in plenary session from 9:00 a.m. to noon for lectures and discussions that outlined the full historical sweep of our topic from pre-Socratic days to current events. As constant threads running through the changing epochs, we paid special attention to the systematic interrelations, within each era, of concepts of freedom in nature, purpose in nature, mind in nature, and the relationship of God to nature. It is a tribute to the zeal of the participants and perhaps also an indication of the quality of the presentations and discussions that attendance was virtually perfect for the entire six weeks of the institute.

Wednesday mornings were reserved for private or small group interviews (for those requesting them) with a series of visiting scholars who came each Tuesday during the middle four weeks, lectured Tuesday afternoon to the participants and other interested members of the university community, and resumed the discussion after dinner and well into the evening on Tuesday, after which intellectual nourishments were reinforced by physical ones. In this stimulating way, the participants met: (1) toward the end of the unit on ancient and medieval thought, with William A. Wallace; (2) early in the unit on modern thought, with Stephen Toulmin; (3) toward the end of the modern unit, with John Compton; and (4) during the unit on contemporary thought, with Charles Hartshorne. One of the important by-products of our receptions for our guests was a strong sense of camaraderie among the participants, a phenomenon that appeared early and grew to important proportions before we were done.

Monday and Thursday afternoons were reserved for the three workshops from which the bibliographies that constitute this book emerged. Each workshop was organized to deal in a sustained manner with one of the three main historical units – ancient and medieval, modern, or contemporary – of the institute's plenary sessions. And since one of the main purposes of the institute was to enrich college and university teaching, the specific task of each workshop – using the library of the University of Georgia, one of the nation's leading research libraries – was to gather, discuss, and annotate bibliographical resources for teaching applications in our areas of study. These are now presented through this book to our colleagues in the wider profession with the hope that they may be of use in many ways, both anticipated and not.

For the institute and the book to have been possible at all, we need to thank the National Endowment for the Humanities and, in particular, three program officers who led us through the complex process of planning (Peter C. Patrikis), application (Barbara A. Ashbrook), and implementation (Elizabeth Welles). During its operation the institute benefitted from a site visit from Dr. Welles, and this book was made possible by her assistance in obtaining permission to use unexpended funds to purchase desktop publishing equipment and software. At the University of Georgia, thanks are especially due to two colleagues in the Department of Philosophy, Bowman Clarke and Frank Harrison, who formed the planning team and, with me, constituted the resident faculty. Dottie Harrison, working evening after pleasant (but hot) summer evening at Frank's side, deserves special kudos for hostess graces far exceeding the call of duty. More officially, but also essentially, we need to recognize the contributions of Dr. Ronald D. Simpson, Director of the Office of Instructional Development, through which the enabling grant was processed, and his capable colleagues, Dr. William Jackson, Associate Director, and Ann Embry, Accountant. They were steadily helpful in large matters and small. Dr. W. Jackson Payne, Dean of the Franklin College of Arts and Sciences, and Dr. Louise McBee, Acting Vice President for Academic Affairs, were constant sources of encouragement and support. Closest to the firing line, Ellen Johnson King, Office Manager of the Department of Philosophy, deserves thanks for taking care of the twenty-six participants – and a number of spouses – through all the practical detail that eating and sleeping and receiving mail and duplicating papers and. . .so on, requires. Mrs. King also typed portions of the manuscripts that make up this book.

It must be said that running an institute like ours, and editing and publishing a book like this, add up to a lot of work. But the hours and pains have been more than compensated by the intellectual and personal rewards accrued. This has been vividly highlighted by the satisfactions in dealing again, after the interval of a year or more, with all the former participants in the process of getting this book into final shape. I find that there is still a special bond among us. We have all worked hard in the interests of good thinking about a significant problem. Now we are glad to imagine the many ways in which our labors may be able to contribute to still more discussions, more discoveries, more pleasures of the mind analogous to those we remember from our summer together in Georgia.

Frederick Ferré

Part One

Curriculum Papers

Workshop on Ancient & Medieval Thought

Frank R. Harrison, III
Workshop Leader

Workshop Leader's Introduction

Frank R. Harrison, III

The members of the Workshop on Ancient and Medieval thought bring a richness of tradition and approach to the exploration, understanding and application of ancient and medieval conceptual schemes to concepts of our own day embedded in a postmodern science and technology. Roman and non-Roman Catholic, and Protestant; lay and cleric; American and European – these backgrounds all added to a diversity fostering a family of interests. This diversity is reflected in the teaching aids produced by the members of this workshop.

NEH Summer Institutes are clearly understood by the National Endowment for the Humanities to have the primary focus of aiding teaching at the undergraduate level. Hence, the goal of this workshop was to create pedagogical tools that, we hoped, would be useful for class lectures and other forms of presentation of basic materials from the ancient and medieval periods. While such a goal might appear simple to achieve, it soon became apparent that it is not.

The members of the workshop first attempted to create class syllabi and outlines of ancient and medieval philosophy for undergraduate classes. Problems to this approach soon became apparent and insurmountable. The heterogeneous nature of the group quickly brought these considerations to the fore: What level of course should be considered? Introduction, advanced, or somewhere in between? Would a semester or quarter term time-frame be assumed? Would ancient be developed in one time-frame and medieval in another, or would it be assumed that both are taught in one term? Would the approach be historical, social, topical, or some combination of these? How would it be determined who, or what, would assume the proportionally greatest amount of time and material covered? Such problems continued to multiply.

Even if all of these problems could be worked out in some general way and syllabi and outlines prepared, still it would be a show of hubris to suppose that many, if any, teachers would ever use them. After all, teachers have their own styles and approaches developing out of their individual personalities and interests, the institutions where they teach, the students they have, and the like. Hence, another approach was sought.

In the end the workshop members searched for what would be the most *USEFUL* teaching tools over a large span of possible applications. The members of the workshop determined to do a careful literature search revolving around most of the main topics of the summer institute: *nature, God, purpose*, and *self* (or in the case of the ancient period, *mind*). This search is limited to those figures who, on the whole, are treated in undergraduate courses in ancient and medieval thought. This approach is not bounded by considerations of time, level of complexity, placement of emphasis, or the like. These issues can be considered and resolved by whomsoever uses the following materials in structuring his or her own courses.

The final pedagogical project of this workshop is, for the most part, a series of notes and references which, if used properly, should save many hours in developing individual courses. The one exception to this procedure is the final paper, "Concepts of Nature and God in the Middle Ages," by the German scholar and teacher, Karl Schmitz-Moormann. This paper serves as a paradigm of how philosophy, culture, science, and technology of an age are interwoven and interdependent upon one another both for their development and understanding. Professor Schmitz-Moormann raises a deceptively simple question: Why is it that clocks are found in medieval churches and not old town halls? One could do well to approach in the same way questions of interest to those studying ancient and medieval philosophy: Why was Thales so interested in water as underlying all things? What was so striking about the craftsman model for Plato? How had the social environment changed so that Stoicism seemed the natural position for a great number of people? In that philosophy is a vital and living thing it cannot be approached, understood or done in a social vacuum. A series of notes and references can be of immense aid in the preparation of lectures, but something like the Schmitz-Moormann approach is needed in order to breathe vigorous life into mere bibliography.

In the end, the success of the offerings of this workshop is in the hands of those who use the following materials. We all, individually and collectively, hope that our efforts are helpful in transmitting ancient and medieval thought while also making it alive and important in the daily lives of students.

One

Concepts of Nature and God in the Pre-Socratics

Walter W. Artus

Nature *(Physis)*

The word, *physis*, is not reliably found in fragments of early Pre-Socratics (except perhaps in Heraclitus).

Aristotle spoke of earliest philosophers as *physikoi* (natural philosophers = students of nature).

For Aristotle "nature" extends to "existent things subject to (substantial) change with an intrinsic principle of their becoming and activities. See Rex Warner, *The Greek Philosophers*, p. 11; also Werner Jaeger, *The Theology of the early Greek philosophers*, p. 8.

According to J. Burnett, early natural philosophers understood by "nature" the everlasting thing out of which the world was made. Burnett, *Early Greek Philosophy*, p. 10. Burnett also says Ionians spoke of their investigations as *peri physeos historie* (science of nature), *Ibid.*, p. 11.

Keeping above remarks on "nature" in mind, read:

a) "Thales, the founder of this type of philosophy, says the principle is water." Aristotle, *Metaphysics*, A, 3 983b 20 (in Milton Nahm's *Selections from early Greek Philosophy*, p. 38).

b) Anaximander: "The first principle and element of existing things is the unlimited." Theophrastus in Simplicius' *In Aristotelis Physicorum Libros Quartos Priores*, 6 r 25 (Nahm, p. 39).

c) Anaximenes: ". . . agrees with him that the essential nature of things is one and infinite, but he regards it as not indeterminate but rather determinate, and calls it air." Theophrastus in Simplicius, *op. cit*. 6 r Doxa 476 (Nahm, p. 43).

"Infinite air is the first principle from which things arise that have come into existence, . . . and gods and things divine." *Ibid.* 7, Doxa 560 (Nahm, p. 44).

d) Pythagoreans "use principles and elements yet stranger than those of the physicists, in that they do not take them from the sphere of sense . . . still they discourse about everything in nature." Aristotle, *Metaphysics*, 1,8, 989b (Nahm, p. 56).

e) According to some writers the following treatises were on and had as title "nature": Anaximander, Heraclitus, Melissus of Samon, Diogenes of Apollonia and Empedocles of Acragas (see Joseph Owens, *A History of Ancient Philosophy*, pp. 13, 43, 90, 104 and 128).

God *(Theos)*

To the early Greek philosophers "*theos*" meant "divine" (a suprahuman and everlasting force or reality). Warner, *op. cit.*, p. 19.

Early Ionians applied the designation "theos" to any "primary substance (ageless and deathless)." Burnett, *op. cit*., p. 14

Cicero in his *De natura Deorum* and St. Augustine in his *De Civitate Dei* thought of the early physicists as the first theologians, repeating what they had found in early Greek sources. Jaeger, *op. cit*., p. 8.

With the above in mind, read:

a) Thales: "Some say that soul is diffused throughout the whole universe; and it may have been this which led Thales to think that all things are full of gods." Aristotle, *De Anima*, 1,2 405a 19 (Nahm, pp. 38/39).

b) Anaximander: "And this (first principle) is eternal and does not grow old, and it surrounds all the worlds." Hippolitus, *Philosophumena*, 6, Doxa 559 (Nahm, p. 39).

c) Anaximenes: "Infinite air is the first principle, from which arise the things that have come and are coming into existence. . . and gods and divine beings, while other things are produced from these." Hippolitus, *op. cit*., 7, Doxa 560 (Nahm, p. 44).

d) Heraclitus: "this world . . . neither god nor any man shaped it, but it ever was and is and shall be everliving fire that kindles by measures and goes out by measures." Fragment. 20 (Nahm, p. 69).

"For all human laws are fostered by one law, which is divine." Fragment 91 (Nahm, p. 73).

e) "Democritus the Abderite supposed the universe to be infinite because it had not been fashioned by any maker. . . The causes of what now exists have no beginning." Plutarch, *Strometeis*, 7 Doxa 581 (Nahm, p. 157).

f) Xenophanes: "But if cattle or lions had hands, so as to paint with their hands and produce works of art as men do, they would paint their gods and give them bodies in form like our own – horses like horses, cattle like cattle. God is one and supreme among gods and men, and not like mortals in body or mind." Fragment 15, 23 (Nahm pp. 84-85).

Purpose *(Telos)*

"And there are some who explain our system and all the worlds by chance . . the heavens and the most divine of visible things arose by chance without a cause, such as plants and animals have." Aristotle, *Physics*, 4, 196 a 24 (Nahm, p. 165).

a) Leucippus: "Nothing occurs at random, but everything for a reason . . . and by necessity." Fragment 2 (Nahm, p. 152).

b) Atomists: ". . . these atoms move at random in the void and collide by chance . . . Thus they produce a world and its contents." Dionysius in Eusebius, *Preparatio Evangelica* XIV, 23, 2.3 (Nahm, p. 158).

Mind *(Nous)*

"Nothing is absolutely separated and distinct. . . except mind." Anaxagoras, Fragment 12 (Nahm, p. 142).

"And when mind began to set things in motion. . . and however much mind set in motion, all this was made distinct." *Ibid.*, Fragment 13 (Nahm, p. 142).

"Then I heard someone who had a book of Anaxagoras. . . out of which he read that mind was the disposer and cause of all, and I was quite delighted at the notion of this. . . As I proceeded, I found my philosopher altogether forsaking mind or any other principle of order, but having recourse to air, and ether, and water, and other eccentricities." Plato, *Phaedo*, 97 B, 98 C (Nahm, p. 143).

Suggested Bibliography:

1. Nahm, Milton, *Selections from Early Greek Philosophy* New York: Appleton-Century-Croft, 1964.

2. Barnes, Jonathan, *The Pre-Socratic Philosophers*, London: Routledge & Kegan Paul, 1979.

3. Benn, Alfred William, *Early Greek Philosophy*, London: Kennicat Press, 1908.

4. Burnett, John, *Early Greek Philosophy*, 4th ed., London: Adam and Charles Black, 1950.

5. Caird, Edward, *The Evolution of Theology in the Early Greek Philosophers*, (vol. 1) 1964.

6. Cleve, Felix M., *The Giants of Pre-Socratic Greek Philosophy*, The Hague: Martinus Nijhoff, 1969.

7. Cornford, F. M., *From Religion to Philosophy*, New York: Harper Torchbooks, 1957.

8. Guthrie, W. K. C., *The Greek Philosophers from Thales to Aristotle*, New York: Harper & Row, 1960.

9. Guthrie, W. K. C., *A History of Greek Philosophy* (Vol. 1 & 2) Cambridge: Cambridge University Press, 1962, 1965.

10. Hack, Roy Kenneth, *God in Greek Philosophy to the Time of Socrates*, New York: Burt Franklin, 1970.

11. Jaeger, Werner, *The Theology of the Early Greek Thinkers*, Oxford: Clarendon Press, 1948.

12. Owens, Joseph, *A History of Ancient Western Philosophy*, New York: Appleton-Century-Croft, 1964.

13. Samburski, Samuel *The Physical World of the Greeks*, New York: The Macmillan Co., 1956.

14. Taylor, Margaret E. J., *Greek Philosophy*, London: Oxford University Press, 1945.

15. Warner, Rex, *The Greek Philosophers*, New York: The New American Library, 1958.

16. Yartz, Frank J., *Ancient Greek Philosophy*, Sourcebook and Perspective, Jefferson, North Carolina: McFarland and Company, 1984.

Two

Plato on God

W. Thomas Schmid

The following outline may be used in a study of Plato's theology, the basic texts including the *Euthyphro*, *Apology*, *Republic*, *Phaedo*, *Symposium*, *Timaeus* and *Laws*. There are strong reasons to study Plato's dialogues as wholes, and not to abstract particular passages for analysis (*Phaedrus* 264c, 270b-277d). Nonetheless, the list of passages below may be used for reference purposes, in order to focus attention on problems in what is today called the philosophy of religion. In a course on this topic, these readings should be supplemented with other readings from the ancient Greek poets and pre-Socratic philosophers. On the "higher mysteries," I recommend R. E. Allen's new book on the *Parmenides*.

The passages are divided into three sections, dealing with Plato's critique of the tradition; Plato's formulation of a new religious orthodoxy/orthopraxy; and Plato's philosophy of the divinity of the human soul, the divine Artisan of nature, and divinity itself. All of the latter topics are extremely difficult, and I would not wish to suggest that this outline represents a comprehensive guide to Plato's views on these matters. It does pull together some readings which are not always seen to be related, and may for that reason be of some value. The first selection indicates the chief readings concerned with the topic indicated. "Also" generally indicates passages specifically associated with the Socratic or philosophical way of life. "Compare" generally indicates passages which offer what at least seem to be alternative or conflicting doctrines, e.g.

the soul as simple vs. the soul as complex, the Artisan as efficient vs. formal or final cause, the God-Being as separate from vs. the God-Being as immanent in the world. "Note" indicates passages which seem to me to be of particular philosophical interest.

I. Critique of the Tradition. Basic texts: *Euthyphro*, *Republic* II-III

A. CRITIQUE OF TRADITIONAL THEOLOGY

See *Euthy.*, esp. 4d-8b, 10a-11b; *Rep.* II-III, esp. 364b-c, 376e-392a, *Laws* X, esp. 899d-907b

Also *Apol.* 21a-23b, *Crat.* 400d, 425c, *Critias* 107b, *Parm.* 134d-e

Compare *Apol.* 35d, *Crito* 51a-c, *Rep.* 363a-e, *Laws* 730a, 843a

Note too *Phaedr.* 246c, *Epis.* 363b; *Tim.* 40d, *Laws* 889e

B. CRITIQUE OF THE TRADITIONAL VIEW OF LIFE AND THE AFTERLIFE

See *Rep.* II-III, esp. 362a-367a, 386a-387d, *Phaedo* 70a, 77e, *Laws* 726a-730a

Also *Apol.* 28b-30b, *Rep.* 386c, 387d-388a & *Gorg.* 526c, *Rep.* 620c

Compare *Rep.* 330d, 363c

Note too *Phaedo* 85e-86d, 86d-88b, 107b, *Craty.* 399d-e, *Epis.* 334e

C. CRITIQUE OF THE TRADITIONAL CONCEPTION OF SERVICE TO THE GODS

See *Euthy.*, esp. 13a-15b, *States.* 290d, *Laws* 905d-907b

Also *Euthy.* 5a, *Apol.* 21a-23b and *Tim.* 27b-d

Compare *Euthy.* 14b, *Rep.* 427b-c, *Laws* 717a-718b, *Epin.* 985d

Note *Euthy.* 12a-e, 15d-16a, Laws 699c, 701a-c, 798b, *Epin.* 977e, 989b

D. SPECIAL TOPICS

1. Divination & prophecy: *Euthy.* 2c, *Apol.* 22c, 39c, *Lach.* 199a, *Prot.* 316d, *Ion* 531b, *Meno* 81a, *Phaedr.* 244a-d, *Tim.* 71a-72b, 91d, *Epin.* 975c

2. Inspiration of poets: *Apol.* 22b, *Ion* 533e-535d, *Meno* 99c, *Symp.* 203a, *Phaedr.* 245a, *Laws* 682a, 719c; compare *Rep.* 365e

II. Formulation of a New Orthodoxy. Basic texts: *Republic* II-III, *Laws* X

A. REFORMS OF THEOLOGY

See *Rep.* II-III, esp. 379a-380c, 380d-383c; also 386a-392a, 612e-613b

Also *Euth.* 6a-c, *Apol.* 21b, 23a, 29e-30b, 41d, *Gorg.* 508a, *Phaedo* 62b-63c

Compare *Laws* 716a, 821a-822d and X, esp. 893b-899d, 899d-905c, 905d-907d, *Epin.* 977a-b, 980a f., esp. 983b, 985a, 988a-b

Note *Rep.* 382a-e & 389b, *Laws* 889e-890d, 891c-892c, *Epin.* 984e, 988c-e

B. A NEW CONCEPTION OF THIS LIFE AND THE AFTERLIFE

See *Rep.* 608b-d, *Phaedo* 107c-d, *Laws* 959a

Myths of the soul's pre-existence, reincarnation and judgment: *Meno* 81a-e, *Phaedo* 72e-77a, *Phaedr.* 246a-253c; *Phaedo* 80a-84a, *Rep.* 614-621d, *Laws* 903d-905c; *Apol.* 40e-41d, *Gorg.* 523a-526d, *Phaedo* 107d-114e

Also *Apol.* 40e-41b, *Gorg.* 526c, *Phaedo* 80d-81a, 114c, *Rep.* 619c, *Phaedr.* 249a, *Tim.* 90a, *Laws* 904d-e, *Epin.* 992b

Compare *Rep.* 414b-415c

Note also *Apol.* 40c (23d), *Rep.* 611c-612a, *Phaedr.* 230a

C. A NEW VIEW OF CORRECT RELIGIOUS SERVICE

See *Apol.* 35d, *Crito* 54c, *Rep.* 383c, 612e-613a, 621c

Compare *Laws* 716a-718d, 726a-732d and 903b

Also *Apol.* 21a-23b and 28e-30b, *Phaedo* 62b-63c, *Phaedr.* 274a

Compare *Rep.* 379a, *Laws* 966c-986a, *Epin.* 980a-c, 985d-986a, 989c-d

Note on *imitatio Dei*: *Euth.* 5b-6a, *Rep.* 388b, 613b, *Phaedr.* 248a, 252e-253a, *Theaet.* 176b-177a; compare *Rep.* 500c; compare *Apol.* 23c, *Gorg.* 490e, *Symp.* 221e; compare *Tim.* 40a-b, 47a-c, 90d, *Laws* 897e-898b

D. SPECIAL TOPICS

1. View of myths: *Euth.* 6a-c, *Prot.* 347c-348a, *Gorg.* 523a, 527a, *Rep.* 377c, 378a, 382c-d, 510a, 595b, 597e-598a, 602b-607a, 621c, *Phaedr.* 229c-e, 245a *Soph.* 235d-236c, *Laws* 645a-b, 682a, 719c, 941b

2. Prayer: see *Alc.II*, 138a-c, *Tim.* 27b-d, *Epis.* 352e-353a; see for examples e.g. *Symp.* 220d, *Phaedr.* 257a, 279b, *Soph.* 249d, Phil. 25b, *Laws* 841c

3. Socrates' sign: *Euthy.* 3b, *Apol.* 31d, 40b-c, 41d, *Alc. I* 105e-106a *Euthyd.* 272e, *Phaedr.* 242c, *Theages* esp. 128d-131a

4. Punishments for impiety: compare *Euthy.* 5a-b, *Apol.* 26b-27e, 35d, and *Laws* 885b-890d, 907d-910d

III. Plato's Religious Philosophy: God and Man, God and Cosmos, God and the Forms

A. INTRODUCTION: PHILOSOPHY AND THE HUMAN SOUL. Basic texts: *Apology*, *Phaedo*, *Republic*, *Phaedrus*

1. CARE OF THE SOUL: esp. *Apology*, *Gorgias*

See *Euth.* 13b, *Apol.* 29d-30b, *Crito* 47d, *Lach.* 185e, *Charm.* 156e, *Alc. I* 132c, *Prot.* 313a-b, *Gorg.* 469b, 470e, 501b, *Phaedo* 82d, 107c, *Rep.* 618d-e, *Symp.* 216a, *Tim.* 87c

Also *Euth.* 9e, *Apol.* 21a-23b, 38a, *Crito* 46b, *Gorg.* 472b-c, 474a 482c, 509a, *Phaedo* 85c-d, 90e-91a

Compare on corruption *Apol.* 23c, *Lach.* 197d, 200b, *Charm.* 164d, *Meno* 71c-72a, 76e and *Phaedr.* 274c-b, *Euthyd.* 277d-278c, *Prot.* 313c-314b, *Gorg.* 483e-484a, *Rep.* 491a-495b, 537e-539c, 559e-561a, 572e-573b, *Symp.* 215e-216b

Note on harm *Apol.* 21d, 30d, 41d, *Gorg.* 466b-467b, 524d-525a, *Phaedo* 83c, *Rep.* 585c-586b, *Theaet.* 177a, *Soph.* 229c & *Laws* 863c, *Laws* 872e, 904e

2. THE NATURE OF THE SOUL: esp. *Phaedo*, *Republic* IV, *Phaedrus*

See on agency/soul: *Crito* 47d, , *Charm.* 156e-157a, *Alc. I* 130a-c, *Prot.* 313a-c, *Gorg.* 493a-c, 524b-525a, *Phaedo* 62b, 67a, 80a, 81a-e, 82c, 93b, 98c-99b, 115d-e, *Crat.* 400c, *Rep.* 353d, 618a-d, *Soph.* 246e-247c

Compare on mind/soul: *Alc. I* 133b-c, *Euthy.* 295e, *Crat.* 407b-c, *Phaedo* 65a-66c, 73c-75b, 78b-79d, 80b *Rep.* 509d-511e, 527e, 534b-d, *Phaedr.* 246d-247e, 248e-250, *Theaet.* 184c-187a, 189e-190a, 191c-f., 197d-f., *Soph.* 248a-249d, *Tim.* 30b, 90a-d, *Phil.* 21d-e

Compare on life & motion/soul: *Charm.* 168e, *Crat.* 399d-400b, *Phaedo* 70d, 85e-86c, 87b-e, 105c-e, 106d, *Rep.* 353d, *Phaedr.* 245c-e, *Tim.* 37c, *Laws* 896a-899b

Compare on parts/soul: *Phaedo*, esp. 62b-69b, 78b-80b vs. *Alc. I* 133b-c, *Meno* 88c; *Gorg.* 493a-b, *Phaedr.* 237d-e; *Rep.* 435b-441c, 580d-581c, 585a-586e, 588b-589a, *Tim.* 67e-72d & 90a-d

Also, on philosophical & other souls: *Gorg.* 526c, *Phaedo* 64c-69d, 80e-81a, 114e, *Rep.* 485a-487a, 490a-d, 535a-536a, *Phaedr.* 248c-249d, 250d-253a, compare *Symp.* 203b-204a and 212a

Note on soul/soul: *Euth.* 9e & *Apol.* 21d, *Charm.* 167a, 168d-e, *Alc. I* 132c-133c, *Meno* 84a-c, *Hip. Maj.* 304d-e, *Phaedo* 74d-e, *Rep.* 523a-524d, 511b-d & 533a-d, *Theaet.* 189e-190a, *Tim.* 37a-c; compare *Lach.* 191d & *Laws* 647d, *Charm.* 155c-e & *Rep.* 432a, *Rep.* 443e-444a, *Rep.* 523a-524d, 511b-d & 533a-d; and compare *Charm.* 168e, *Phaedr.* 245e, *Tim.* 37b, *Laws* 896a, 898e-899a

Note too *Phaedo* 80b, *Symp.* 207e-208b, *Rep.* 611b-612a, *Phaedr.* 246a, 270c-271a (esp. 270c), *Tim.* 72d

3. THE CONVERSION OF THE SOUL: esp. *Republic* VII, *Symposium* 198-222

See *Apol.* 29d-30b, *Crito* 49d, *Gorg.* 481b-c *Phaedo* 63e-69d, 82c-84b, *Rep.* 514a-519d, 521c f., 585c-d, *Symp.* 210a-212a, *Parm.* 135c-136c, *Tim.* 90c-d, *Laws* 966a-968a, *Epin.* 991e-992a, *Epis.* 341b-d, 344a-b

On Socrates, see: *Apol.* 21a-23b, *Hip. Maj.* 304d-e, *Phaedo* 96a-100a, *Symp.* 201c-210a, *Parm.* 127b f., esp. 130e

Compare *Lysis* 221d-222a, *Theages* 128d-131a, *Symp.* 215d-219d, 221d-222a, *Phaedr.* 250d-253c, 253d-256e

Note also on philosophical method: *Lach.* 187e-188b, *Hip. Maj.* 304d-e, *Gorg.* 464b, *Meno* 80c-d, 84a-c, *Phaedr.* 270b-272b, *Theaet.* 150b-151d, *Soph.* 228c-230e

4. ARGUMENTS FOR THE IMMORTALITY OF THE SOUL: esp. *Phaedo*

See argument from agency: *Phaedo* 80a, 92e-95a, *Rep.* 608d-611a

Compare argument from recollection: *Meno* 85b-86b, *Phaedo* 72e-77a, 78b-79e, 91c-92e

Compare arguments from life, self-motion: *Phaedo* 70d-72d, 102b-107d, *Phaedr.* 245c-e, *Laws* 893a-899d

Note too: *Phaedo* 70d, 76c-d, 76e, 80b, 107b, *Rep.* 611b-612a

Note on creativity-immortality: *Symp.* 204e & 206a, 206b-207a and 207d-208b, 208c-d & 209a-e, 212a *Phaedr.* 276-277a, also *Phaedo* 79d, *Tim.* 90c

B. THEOLOGY: GOD AND NATURE.
Basic texts: *Timaeus*, *Laws* X

1. COSMOS, PLAN, WORLD-SOUL

See on real and ideal cosmos: *Rep.* 529a-531c, *Phaedo* 75a, 96a-107a, 109a-111c, *Tim.* 27e-29d, 29e-30b, 30c-31b, 37d-38b, 39e, 53e, 56c, 69b, 91d, 92c; *Laws* 897e-898b; compare *Symp.* 206e-208c

Compare also on ideal cosmos: *Tim.* 30c-d, 39e-40a, 41e-42b, 47a-e, 87e, 88b-90d, 41c-d & 91a-92c, *Soph.* 248e-249a

On world-soul, see: *Tim.* 34c-37a, *Laws* 716a, 896a-899d (esp. 897a) *Phil.* 30a-e, *Epin.* 983a-e, 988d-e; compare *States.* 269c-273d

On intelligence in or of: *Tim.* 30b, 35a-36e, 37a-c, 38e, 40a-b, *Laws* 821b-822c, 898a-b, *Epin.* 978c-979a, 982a-e, 986c, 988b,

991d-992a, and *Tim.* 53b, 56c, 69b-c, note *Epin.* 982a-e; compare also *Tim.* 37a-c, 90d, *Epin.* 988b; compare *Tim.* 29e-30a, 46d-e, 47b-d, 53b, 68e, 75e, 89a, 90d, compare to these *Phaedo* 97c-99c

Compare *Laws* 889a-890a, 891b-892c

Note on 'cosmology' *Rep.* 529a-530c, *Tim.* 29b-d, 46d-e, 48c-d, 51c-52a, 59c-d, 68d, 72d, also *Phaedo* 97c-99c

Note on contemplation of cosmos *Tim.* 36e, 37d, 47a-c, 90a-d, 91d *Epin.* 978d, 988b, 991e-992a, compare *Phaedo* 101c, *Rep.* 525d, 527a-b, 529d, *Tim.* 37e-38b, 51c-e, 52b-c, *Epin.* 990c

2. COSMOGONY, RECEPTACLE, WORLD-BODY

See *Tim.* 34c-36d, 31b-34b, 36d-40d, 41d-e & 69c; 42d-43a & 44d-45b

Compare *Tim.* 52d-55c, 57d-61c, 69c-79a, 91a-d; also 31b, 34a with 35c, 36d

Compare too *Laws* 889a-890a, 891c-e, *Prot.* 320c-328c, *States.* 274a-d, *Tim.* 47a-b, *Epin.* 977c-978a

On the pre-existent elements from which phenomenal cosmos created, compare *Tim.* 49b-e, 50c, 52c, 52e-53b with 53c, 54a-55c (compare too 31b-32c)

On the receptacle, compare *Tim.* 50a-51b, 52b-c and 52e, 53a (compare *Laws* 893b-895b; also compare *Tim.* 37a-c)

Note *Tim.* 52b-c (cf. *Phaedo* 73c-e)

3. ARGUMENTS FOR THE EXISTENCE OF A CREATOR-GOD, WORLD-SOUL

See for cosmological argument *Tim.* 27e-28c

See for teleological argument *Tim.* 28a-29a

Compare argument for first mover, *Laws* 894e-895a; argument from non-motion, *Laws* 895a-b; and argument from soul as universal cause, *Laws* 896b-e, *Epin.* 983d-e; argument for good soul as cause of universe's motion, *Laws* 896e-898c, *Epin.* 988d-e; argument from magnitude of heavenly motion, *Epin.* 983a-b

Compare argument from analogy of man to cosmos, *Phil.* 29d-30b

4. DISCUSSION OF THE NATURE OF THE CREATOR-GOD

See on Creator as agent *Tim.* esp. 27e-29a, 30a-d, 41a-d, 53b-55a, 69c & e.g. 32b, 34b, 35a-36e, 37c-d, 38c-d, 40a-b, see too 47c, 73b-75b, c-d, 76c, 78b-c but compare 69c; *Rep.* 507c, 530a, 597b-c, *Soph.* 265c, 266b, *Phil.* 23d, 26e-27b, 30a-d, note 61a & compare *Symp.* 196e, 199c-207a, 208a-b, note too *Tim.* 30a on His will

Compare on Creator as formal/final cause *Tim.* esp. 29e, 46c-e, 47e-48a, 68e-69a, 76d & e.g. 50d, 71a, d-e, 74b-c, e, 75b-c, 76b, d, compare 78c-e and 79a-e; *Phil.* 27a & *Phaedo* 97c-98c, *Symp.* 207a-208b, 211b

Note contrast of God as cause of gods & gods as cause of weaving together the mortal & immortal and governing them *Tim.* 41c, 42d-43a, 68e, 69c (but note 41a and compare 68e); *Laws* 897a, *Epin.* 979a-b

See on Creator's goodness & rational nature, *Tim.* 29a, 29e-30a, 37c (cf. *Tim.* 30b, *Phil.* 21d,), 41a-b, 42b *States.* 273b-c; *Tim.* 30a-c, 38c, 39e, 41c, 51e & e.g. 42e, 76d-e, *Laws* 897b, *Phil.* 29a, 30b, d-e, also *Euth.* 10a-11b

See on Creator's power & knowledge *Tim.* 28c-29a, 30a, b-c, 41a-b & 69c, 68d, 72d; compare his limits esp. *Tim.* 47e-48b, e.g. 32b, 42a, 52d-53a, 53b, 56c, 89c, *States.* 269e, these to 30a, 41a-b (essential goodness); compare also e.g. *Tim.* 27e-28a, 29a, 37e-38b, 52a to *Rep.* 597c-d

Note on man's knowledge/ignorance of God *Tim.* 28c, 34c, 37e-38b, 43e-44a, 46d-e, 52b-c, 68d

5. SPECIAL TOPICS

a. THE PROBLEM OF EVIL

See *Craty.* 432c, *Rep.* 379c-380b, 597a, *Theaet.* 176a, *Soph.* 240a, *States.* 273b, *Phil.* 16d, 26b, also *Phaedo* 66b-e, 81b, *Tim.* 86e

Compare *Phaedr.* 245c, *Laws* 803e, 892a, 896a, *Tim.* 30a, 46e, 47e-48a, 56c, 68e with *Laws* 896d-897d, esp. 897a-d

See also *Phaedo* 62b, 81d, 82a-83c and *Prot.* 326e, *Gorg.* 469b Note *Tim.* 39e, 41c, compare 42a-d

Note *Rep.* 617c, *Tim.* 47e, *Laws* 741a, compare *Laws* 901e-903d

b. MIRACLES AND THE NECESSARY IN NATURE

See *States.* 274a, *Laws* 741a, 901d, implied absence of intervention *Tim.* 41a-d, 71a-72b, 47e ff. on necessity, cf. also on prayer; on the necessary in nature, compare *Laws* 818b-d, *Epin.* 982b

c. FREEDOM AND DETERMINISM

See on freedom of mind, will: *Apol.* 21d, *Crito* 46b, *Prot.* 352a-361a, *Lach.* 191c-192c, compare 192e-194a, 194c-196a, *Gorg.* note 466b-467a, 491d, 493a-c, 481c-e, 513b & *Symp.* 216a, Crat. 403a, also *Phaedo* 64a-69a, 80a, 83c, 94b-e, 98c-99c, *Rep.* note 366c-d, 386b, 429a-432a, also

443d-444a & 514a-517a, 518a, 519a-b, compare 537e-539a, 560d-561e, 572d-572c & 579a-e, 589d-e, note 618c-e, *Soph.* 228e, 253c-d, *States.* 274a-d, *Tim.* 47c, 87b, 88b-c, 89e, 90c-d, *Laws* 644d-645b, 647c-e, 904b-e, 963e, *Epis.* 354e

Compare *Rep.* 515e, 619b-620e, also 414d-415c, 491a, 494a, *Tim.* 39e, 41c, 86e-87b, *Laws* 644d, 803c & note 889d, 901e-903d

Note on choice of life *Gorg.* 487c, 493c, 500c-d, 512e, *Rep.* 347e, 352d, 617e-618e

Note God not to blame *Rep.* 617e *States.* 274d, *Tim.* 42d, *Laws* 904b-c, but compare 901e-903d

C. THE "HIGHER MYSTERIES": DIVINITY AND THE FORMS

1. THE EXISTENCE AND SEPARATENESS OF THE DIVINE

See on god/gods *Phaedo* 63b, 111b, *Symp.* 203a, *Phaedr.* 246a-247e, *States.* 272e; *Tim.* 29a (but note 30a, 41a-b); *Laws* 896e-899d (note 898a, 898e-899a); against atheism, see *Theaet.* 176e-177a, *Laws* 888c, 889e

Compare on Ideas *Phaedo* 65d-66a, 74a-75d, 100a-103c, *Rep.* 475e- 476a, 510e-d, 524a-526a, 596a, *Crat.* 439a-440b, *Parm.* 128e-129a *Tim.* 27e, 30c-d, 51c-52a, *Epis.* 342a-343a; against non-reality of Ideas, see *Soph.* 249b-c, *Parm.* 135b-c; on problem of separateness, *Parm.* esp. 130a-135d, 137c-142a

2. THE ACTIVITY OF THE DIVINE

On gods/God knowing/thinking, see *Apol.* 23a, *Symp.* 204a, *Phaedr.* 247a-b, note esp. 249c,d *Soph.* 248e-249a, knows truth by contact *Tim.* 37a-c, 68d, *Phil.* 33a-b *Epin.* 988b, cf. also

Phaedo 66a, 79a, *Symp.* 217a, 222a, 220c-d and compare *Parm.* 135a, *Soph.* 253c-e and *Tim.* 68d, *Phil.* 62a-b; ideal and sensible world-order *Tim.* 37a-c, knows Himself *Epin.* 988b

Compare on Ideas as cause of knowing *Phaedo* 73c-76c, esp. 76d-e, 99e, 100a-102b, *Craty.* 439a-440b, *Rep.* 476e, 479a, 508d, 511a-b, 516a, 527a, note *Phaedr.* 249c, *Parm.* 135a-b, *Soph.* 249b-c, *Phil.* 58a-59c; on Idea of Good as cause of beingness & being-known of objects of knowledge *Rep.* 507a-509c, 516b-c, 517b-c (compare 597c-d), 585c

On gods/God willing/loving/causing, see *Symp.* 197c, perfect love 206c, 212a, 215b, 216d-e (contrast eros 201a-c, 203b-204a, 215e-216c, 217b-219e), love = divine possession *Phaedr.* 249c-e, Godlike love *Phaedr.* 252e-253a, b, esp. *Tim.* 29e-30a, 33d, 37c, 41c, 47a, 53b, 90a, *Epin.* 988b; God creator of souls, life, esp. rational soul *Tim.* 34b-35b, 41c, lesser through gods, *Tim.* 41d, 69c-d, *Epin.* 983b

Compare on Ideas as cause of willing/loving *Phaedo* 66a, 74d-75b, *Rep.* 475b, e, 476d, 509a, 523b, 584b, 524e, note 585d, 586e, *Symp.* 210a-212a, 217a & *Phaedr.* 248b-c, 250a-d, beloved image of Idea *Phaedr.* 252c-d, *Phil.* 64b, 3 Ideas of Good = cause of goodness of mixture *Phil.* 65a, the Good as cause of 'existence and being' of Ideas *Rep.* 509b, 517c, even of sensibles 516b-c, 517c

3. THE DIVINITY OF THE DIVINE

See on modes of reality *Phaedo* 78b-79b, *Rep.* 509e-511e, 519a-b, 32a-b, 534a-b, 585c, *Symp.* 202e-203a, *Soph.* 237a-256d, note 238a-c, 246a-249d, 250b, esp. 255c, *Tim.* 35a, 68d, compare 35a-b & 52a-b, 36d-e, 42 *Phil.* 23c-27c, 30e (but note 27a), 53d-54a *Epis.* 342a-343c

See on maximum possible goodness & complete reality *Euth.* 13c, *Rep.* 379a-b, 381b-c, 387d & 388c, 585a-d , *Symp.* 202c, 204a, on divine mind esp. *Phaedr.* 249c, *Soph.* 248e-249a, compare 253c-d & *Tim.* 68d, *Laws* 901e, 903c, *Phil.* 22c, 33a-b, 52a-b, 60c-e, 63a-c (compare *Tim.* 37c & above on divine love)

Compare *Phaedo* 75a-d, note *Rep.* 506e, 509b, 518c, 532c, & esp. 585c, *Symp.* 211a, *Phaedr.* 247e, *Parm.* 131b (note analogy not = to Sun), 132d *Soph.* 246b-c, *Tim.* 33b, *Phil.* 27e-28a, 59c, 60b-c, 66a

See on self-identity in themselves *Rep.* 380d-381c, *States.* 269d, 272e, *Phaedr.* 247a & *Craty.* 401b-c, *Phaedr.* 247a, also 252c-253a, *Tim.* 31a-b, 33b, *Laws* 897c-898b

Compare *Phaedo* 74a-75d, 78d-e, 101c-d, note *Rep.* 524e, 597d, *Symp.* 211b, *Soph.* 248a, 250c, 254d, 255c (compare 255b), *Tim.* 27e, 29c, 30c-31b, 51a, compare at level of Ideas *Soph.* 251d-256e, esp. 253d, 255b-e, 256d-e, compare *Parm.* 139d-e, 146a-147b, 163c-d

See on immortality, eternity & 'placelessness' *Phaedo* 106b-d, *Symp.* 202d, 203e, world-soul 'older' than world-body, *Tim.* 34c, *Laws* 892a, note rational world-soul knows, but is not in time *Tim.* 36e-38b, 89a, 90d, cf. also *Soph.* 249a-c, compare *Phil.* 33a-b; gods in heaven, *Phaedr.* 246e-247c, note 248a, cosmos not in place, *Tim.* 34b, see world-soul is 'in' body & vice-versa & omnipresent *Tim.* 30b, 34b, note 52b-c, *Laws* 898e-899a

Compare on eternity of Ideas, Eternal Creature *Tim.* 28a, 29a, 37e-38a, 38b, 52a, 52b-c, compare *Parm.* 140e-141d, 151e-155c, 155e, esp. 140a, 152a, 155e, 156a, 162e-163b; on 'placelessness' see *Rep.* 592a-b, *Symp.* 211a, *Phaedr.* 247c, *Parm.* 131a-c, 138a-b, compare 145b-e, 151a, 163e

See on impassibility *Rep.* 377e-378a, 378d, 388c, 389a, 390b-c, *Phil.* 33a-b, but compare *Apol.* 41d, *Laws* 899e-904c, 906d-e, *Theaet.* 153c-d (compare *Rep.* 509b), *Soph.* 248e-249a & *Tim.* 37a, 37c

Compare *Phaedo* 78d-e, 97a-b, 101c-d *Rep.* 509b, 527a-b, *Parm.* 138b-139b *Soph.* 250a-c, 254d, compare 248e & 249b-c, compare *Parm.* 145e-146a, 156a-c, 162b-163b

Three

Aristotle on God and Nature

David K. Clark

God:

Metaphysics VI, 1—The three sciences—natural science, mathematics and theology—deal with objects which are movable (physical objects), which are immovable but inseparable from matter (mathematical objects), and which are immovable and separable from matter (the divine) respectively.

Metaphysics XII, 7—God is described as eternal, good, active mind, dispenser of life, immovable, separable from sensation.

Metaphysics XII, 6; *Physics* VIII, 6—Aristotle develops arguments for the Unmoved Mover. The Unmoved Mover exhibits unity, simplicity, pure actuality, and moves everything else by the lure of final causality.

Eudemian Ethics VII, 14—God, the divine, is what moves everything both in the individual soul (including human thinking) and in the universe.

Politics VII, 1 – Humans are happy according to the degree of wisdom and wise action just as the gods are happy by virtue of their own nature.

Metaphysics XII, 9 – The dilemma of thought: if God does not think, he is like one who is asleep; if he does think, he is dependent on other things and will think changing things. God's "thinking is a thinking about thinking," which means that the thinker becomes one with its object (abstracted from matter) so that "thought has itself for its object"

Metaphysics XII, 8 – The forty-nine or fifty-five spheres, substances which, according to the "inspired" myth, are gods.

Nature:

Metaphysics V, 4 – Aristotle gives five definitions of "nature."

Physics II, 1 – Natural objects move by virtue of their own animation, not by something else or accidentally (in contrast to art). (Cf. *Physics* I, 7-8; II, 1-3, 8-9; *Poetics* 1-4.)

Physics V, 6; III, 1 – Nature is the principle of motion; different objects have different "natural" motions.

Physics IV, 1, 8; VII, 4; *On the Heavens* I, 2-3, 7-8 – Natural motions are different from compulsory motions.

Rhetoric I, 10 – If something happens "by nature," it is caused by a fixed and internal cause.

On the Soul II, 4 – "Nature" as a character of a thing; e.g., it is the nature of living things to reproduce other like living things. (Cf. *Metaphysics* IV, 1.)

Parts of Animals II, 1—The characters or natures of things are endowed for an end.

Physics I, 4—Nature is not random.

Parts of Animals II, 1—Aristotle uses "nature" to mean everything that exists.

Purpose:

On the Heavens I, 4; *Progression of Animals* 8—God and nature do nothing without purpose.

Physics II, 8—Things in nature operate for an end. Animals are the best evidence of this for they cannot deliberate, and yet they reveal purpose in their actions. Monstrosities fail to achieve an end, but do show that purpose was attempted even though not attained.

Parts of Animals II, 14-15—Aristotle gives examples of things which exhibit purpose—hair, eyebrows, and eyelashes.

Parts of Animals I, 5—In the works of nature orderliness and purpose are found in the highest degree. (Cf. *Generation of Animals* II, 6—nature even contrives the synchronizing of old age and the wearing down of teeth.)

Parts of Animals II, 1—Matter exists for the objects formed out of it as bricks exist for the house.

Parts of Animals IV, 10—Nature is not wasteful; it gives organs to animals which can actually use them (e.g., hands to intelligent humans) as any prudent person would do.

Parts of Animals IV, 12 – Nature makes organs for functions, not functions for organs. (Note how the evolutionary understanding of this relation would be opposite of Aristotle's).

Physics II, 4-7 – Aristotle interprets chance and luck in view of his purposive view of nature. (Cf. *Politics* I, 11.)

Mind:

On the Soul I, 3 – Thought is an activity of the soul; neither the mind nor the soul has magnitude.

On the Soul II, 3 – "Soul" has various connotations according to the kind of organism under consideration. In humans, "soul" is connected to the power of thought.

On the Soul III, 4-5 – The mind cannot have a certain quality or it would not be able to think without hindrance; in a sense, it is not any real thing before it thinks. The mind cannot be mixed with the body. The mind is a blank tablet.

On the Generation of Animals II, 3 – Reason is divine and has no connection with bodily things.

Nicomachean Ethics X, 7 – Humans are most basically intellectual beings; this is the divine element. Happiness comes from the development of the intellect.

Eudemian Ethics VII, 15 – The rational aspect of humans is both divine and good.

Four

Hellenistic-Roman Philosophy: A Bibliography

Dennis Temple and Justin Nolan, O.S.B.

Introduction

There were three major schools in this era (c. 320 B.C. - 380 A.D.): the Epicureans, the Stoics, and the Skeptics. Both the Academy and the Lyceum existed through this period and kept alive the thought of Plato and Aristotle respectively, but for the most part they were not centers of creative thought. The academy was a center of skepticism for about 100 years under the headship of Carneades, Arcesilas and others; it returned to orthodox Platonism at about the time of Cicero (c. 50 B.C). Towards the end of this era Neo-Platonism was growing in significance (it influenced Philo of Alexandria, St. Augustine and other religious thinkers). This bibliography is confined to the three major schools.

Very little survives of the voluminous literary output of these three schools. Epicurus is said to have written nearly 300 books; of these nothing survives but a few fragments and a few quotations preserved in other authors. The only work of later Epicureans that survives more or less intact is *De Rerum Natura (On Nature)* by the Roman author, Lucretius (c. 50 B.C.). As for the Stoics, no work of Zeno of Citium survives, and of the chief Stoics of the Hellenistic era (Cleanthes and Chrysippus) only fragments. The Roman Stoics are represented only by works on practical ethics from Epictetus, Marcus Aurelius, and Seneca. The founder of Skepticism, Pyrrho, was said to have written nothing; the same is true of some other prominent Skeptics (e.g., Carneades). Ironically, we have some fairly large works from this school: Cicero's *De Natura Deorum (On the nature of Gods)* and *Academica (The Academics)*, and especially the four volumes of Sextus Empiricus (c. 200 A.D.), including *Outlines of Pyrrhonism*, *Against the Logicians*, *Against the Physicists*, and *Against the Ethicists*.

Because very few really primary sources have come down to us, scholars are forced to depend heavily on a few secondary sources which have survived from the ancient work. The main ones are various works of Cicero (including those mentioned above) and Diogenes Laertius, *Lives of Eminent Philosophers* (*circa* 200 A.D.).

Epicureans

1. Diogenes Laertius, Book X, "Epicurus." On physics, see the "letter to Heroditus" (articles 35-83) and the "letter to Pythocles" (articles 84-116). See also the "Sovran Maxims," especially numbers 1 and 11.

The bliss of Gods: "We are bound to believe that in the sky revolutions, solstices, eclipses, risings and settings and the like, take place without the ministration or command, either now or in the future, of any being [god] who at the same time enjoys perfect bliss along with immortality. For troubles and anxieties and feelings of anger and partiality do not accord with bliss, but always imply weakness and fear and dependence." [77]

The purpose of science: "In the first place, remember that like everything else, knowledge of celestial phenomena... has no other end in view than peace of mind and firm conviction." [86] "If we had never been molested by alarms at celestial and atmospheric phenomena, nor by the misgiving that death somehow affects us, nor by neglect of the proper limits of pains and desires, we should have had no need to study natural science." [142]

2. Cicero, *De Natura Deorum*, Book I, Articles 18-56. For the Epicurean view of nature, see especially articles 43-56.

Divine bliss: "You Stoics are also fond of asking us, Balbus, what is the mode of life of the gods and how they pass their days. The answer is, their life is the happiest conceivable.... God is entirely inactive and free from all ties of occupation; he toils not neither does he labor, but he takes delight in his own wisdom and virtue, and knows with absolute certainty that he will always enjoy pleasures at once consummate and everlasting." [51]

3. Lucretius, *On Nature*.

The swerve: "While the first bodies are being carried downwards by their own weight in a straight line through the void , at times quite uncertain and uncertain palaces, they swerve a little.... [If they did not swerve,] all would fall downwards. . ., no collision would take place and. . .nature would never have produced anything. [Book II, 216] "If the first beginnings do not make by swerving a beginning of motion such as to break the decrees of fate, ...whence comes this free will in all the living creatures...?" [Book II, 251]

Laws of nature: "But do not think that animals only are held by these laws, for the same principle holds all things apart by their limits." [Book II, 718] (Note: When Lucretius talks about laws of nature he uses either *lex* [statute, law] or *foedus* [ordinance, decree, treaty]. Both words come from Latin roots which mean "to bind.")

Sufficiency of nature: "If you hold fast to these convictions, nature is seen to be free at once and rid of proud masters, herself doing all herself of her own accord, without the help of the gods." [Book II, 1090]

Death: "Therefore, death is nothing to us, it matters not one jot, since the nature of the mind is understood to be mortal. . . . When we shall no longer be, when the parting shall have come about between body and spirit from which we are compacted in one whole, then sure nothing at all will be able to happen to us, who will no longer be, or to make us feel. . . ." [Book III, 830] (Note: For Lucretius the spirit is material, composed of very smooth and round atoms dispersed throughout the body.)

Stoics

1. Diogenes Laertius, Book VII, Chapter 1, "Zeno." A General account of Stoicism is given in articles 38-160. The physical doctrine is covered in articles 132-160. See also Chapter 5, "Cleanthes," and Chapter 7, "Chrysippus."

The cosmos: "[The Stoics] hold that there are two principles in the universe, the active principle and the passive. The passive principle, then, is a substance without quality, i.e. matter, whereas the active is the reason inherent in this substance, that is God." [VII, 134] "The world, in their view, is ordered by reason and providence. . . . Thus, then, the whole world is a living being endowed with soul and reason. . . ." [VII, 139]

God: "The deity, they say, is a living being, immortal, rational, perfect or intelligent in happiness, admitting nothing evil [into him], taking providential care of the world and all that therein is, but he is not of human shape. He is, however, the artificer of the universe and, as it were, the father of all. . . ." [VII, 147]

Nature: "Nature is defined as a force moving of itself, producing and preserving in being its offspring. . . within definite periods. Nature, they hold, aims both at utility and pleasure, as is clear from the analogy with human craftsmanship." [VII, 149]

2. Cicero, *De Natura Deorum* Book II. Stoic proofs for the existence of God are found in articles 4-44; the nature of God is covered in 45-72; an extensive discussion of divine providence is found in articles 73-153; finally, articles 154-167 discuss the providential care of human beings.

Providence: "The nature of the world itself is styled by Zeno not merely 'craftsmanlike' but actually 'a craftsman,' whose foresight plans out the work to serve its use and purpose in every detail. . . . Such being the nature of the world-mind, it can therefore be correctly designated as prudence or providence. . .; and this providence is chiefly directed and concentrated upon three objects, namely to secure for the world, first, the structure best fitted for survival; next, absolute completeness; but chiefly, consummate beauty and embellishment of every kind." [II, 58]

Design: "But if the structure of the world in all its parts is such that it could not have been better whether in point of utility or beauty, let us consider whether this is the result of chance, or whether on the contrary the parts of the world are in such a condition that they could not possibly have cohered together if they were not controlled by intelligence and divine providence. . . . When you see a statue or a painting, you recognize the exercise of art; when you observe from a distance the could of a ship, you do not hesitate to assume that is motion is guided by reason and by art; when you look at a sundial or a water-clock, you infer that it tells the time by art and not by chance; how then can it be consistent to suppose that the world, which includes both the works of art in question, the craftsmen who made them, and everything else besides, can be devoid of purpose and of reason?" [II, 87] (Paley take note!)

Skeptics

1. Diogenes Laertius, Book IX, Chapter 11, "Pyrrho." A summary of the ten modes of Aenesidemus is found in articles 79-88; the five modes of Agrippa are mentioned in 88-89. Most of the chapter consists of anecdotes allegedly drawn form the life of Pyrrho; it has little philosophical content apart from the brief discussion of the modes (Note: Modes were ways of attacking views of the dogmatists so as to achieve the goal of classic skepticism: non-belief, and through it peace of mind.)

Imperturbability: "[Pyrrho] would maintain the same composure at all times, so that, even if you left him when he was in the middle of speech, he would finish what he had to say with no audience but himself. . . . Once when Anaxarchus fell into a slough, he passed by without giving any help, and while others blamed him, Anaxarchus praised his indifference. . . ." [article 63]

More imperturbability: "When a mad dog rushed at him and terrified him, he answered his critic that it was not easy entirely to strip oneself of human weakness. . . . They say that, when. . .salves and surgical and caustic remedies were applied to a wound he had sustained, he did not so much as frown. . . . When his fellow passengers on board a ship were all unnerved by a storm, he kept calm and confident, pointing to a little pig in the ship that went on eating, and telling them that such was the unperturbed state in which the wise man should keep himself." [articles 66; 67; 68] (Note: There is good reason to believe that Pyrrho went to India with the army of Alexander; it has been suggested that his philosophy was influenced by the so-called "gymnosophists," "naked sages" – perhaps Buddhists or Jains – that the Greeks met there.)

2. Cicero, *De Natura Deorum* Book I, articles 58-124; Book III. The last half of Book I is a skeptical attack on Epicurean theology; Book III is an attack on Stoic theology. Of particular interest is the last part of Book III (articles 65-95) which contains strong objections to the Stoic belief in the governance of the world by divine providence.

Against Epicurus' argument from assent: "You said that a sufficient reason for admitting that the gods exist was the fact that all nations and races of mankind believe it. But this argument is both inconclusive and untrue. In the first place, . . . I think that there are many nations so uncivilized and barbarous as to have no notion of any gods at all. Again, did not Diagoras, called the Atheist, and later Theodorus openly deny the divine existence?" [I, 62]

Against the Epicurean swerve: "This is a very common practice with your school. You advance a paradox, and then, when you want to escape censure, you adduce in support of it some absolute impossibility. . . . For instance, Epicurus saw that if the atoms traveled downwards by their own weight, we should have no freedom of the will, since the motion of the atoms would be determined by necessity. He therefore invented a device to escape from determinism. . . : he said that the atom while travelling vertically downward by the force of gravity makes a very slight swerve to one side. This defence discredits him more than if he had to abandon his original position." [I, 69]

Against the Epicurean view of divine happiness: "'God is engaged (they say) in ceaseless contemplation of his own happiness, for he has no other object for his thoughts.' I beg of you to realize in your imagination a vivid picture of a deity solely occupied for all eternity in reflecting 'What a good time I am having! How happy I am!' And yet I can't see how the happy god of yours is not to fear destruction, since he is subjected without a moment's respite to the buffeting and jostling of a horde of atoms that eternally assail him, while from his own person a ceaseless stream of images is given off. Your god is therefore neither happy or eternal." [I, 114] (Note: Epicureans held that gods were material beings, and that all material beings constantly "evaporate" images which can then be perceived by others. Images of the gods were supposed to be perceived in dreams.)

Against the Stoic "proof" that the world is rational: "The whole of this topic of yours was expanded tersely, and as you thought effectively, by the famous old syllogism of Zeno. Zeno puts the argument thus: 'That which is rational is superior to that which is not rational; but nothing is superior to the world; therefore the world is rational.' If you accept this conclusion, you will go on to prove that the world is perfectly able to read a book: for following in Zeno's footsteps you will be able to construct a syllogism as follows: 'That which is literate is superior to that which is illiterate; but nothing is superior to the world: therefore the world is literate.'" [III, 22]

Against Stoic providence: "However, we are dwelling too long on a point that is perfectly clear. Telamo despatches the whole topic of proving that the gods pay no heed to man in a single verse: 'For if they cared for men, good men would prosper and bad men would come to grief; but this is not so.' Indeed the gods ought to have made all men good, if they really cared for the human race; or failing that, they certainly at all events ought to have cared for the good." [III, 79] (There follows a long list of good men who suffered injustice or otherwise came to grief.)

3. Sextus Empiricus. The quotation here is from a book of selections from his writings (taken from *Outlines of Pyrrhonism* and *Against the Physicists*) edited by Philip Hallie. (This is available in a paperback edition from Hackett.)

Against Stoic providence: "He who says that God exists either affirms or denies his forethought for the things in the world, and if he affirms it, he affirms it either for all things or some things. But if he had forethought for all things, there would be neither any bad thing nor any evil in the world. Therefore, God will not be said to have forethought for all things. But if he has forethought for some things, why for some things and not for others? For either he has both the will and the power to think of all things beforehand, or he has the will but not the power, or the power but not the will, or neither the will nor the power. But if he had both the will and the power, he would have forethought for all things, but *ex hypothesi* he does not forethink all things; therefore he does not have both the will and the power.... And if he has the will but not the power, he is weaker than that which is the cause of his inability.... But it is against our conception of God that he should be weaker than anything. But if he has the power of forethought for all things but not the will, he will be considered malicious. And if he has neither the will nor the power, he is both malicious and weak. But to say this about God is impiety. Therefore God has not forethought for the things in the world." [pp. 177-178] (Note: The point of this is merely to counter the Stoic arguments. As a good Skeptic, Sextus neither affirms nor denies anything in his own right.)

Five

Concepts of Nature and God in the Middle Ages

Karl Schmitz-Moormann

In *Adventures of Ideas*, Whitehead observes that "in each age of the world distinguished by high activity there will be found at its culmination some profound cosmological outlook, implicitly accepted, impressing its own type on the current springs of action. This ultimate cosmology is only partly expressed, and the details of such expression issue into derivative specialized questions of violent controversy."[1] If Whitehead's judgment is correct, then our understanding of cosmology and nature in the Middle Ages can hardly be based on reading the traditionally quoted philosophical texts from the Summas. These highly abstract texts rarely give us any insight into the understanding of the concrete world of that time and the way their thinking about God was related to this concrete world of theirs. In this context it might be worthwhile to remember that philosophy in that time, when it was considered to be the *ancilla theologiae*, had three essential parts, namely ethics, logic and physics (and no metaphysics).[2] When we treat the thinking of the Middle Ages we mostly forget about their physics, taking for granted the enlightenment prejudice that no really scientific work, i.e. thinking based on observation, was part of the Middle Ages.

To overcome this rationalist and neoscholastic prejudice it might be interesting to turn towards the concrete "fossils" of the Middle Ages whose existence philosophers have a tendency to take as without real importance; at least they hardly refer to them. I think especially of the numerous great cathedrals which are strangely enough still in everyday use. The workmanship in their creation implied a good at least practical knowledge of physics and statics. And in some of these cathedrals you find those rather late Middle Ages astronomical clocks whose design boggles even the modern watchmaker.

We are mostly used to admiring these clocks as pieces of extremely high watchmaker-art. But in our context the by far more interesting question is what these clocks are meant for in the church. They do not seem to us a special enticement to prayer, and they normally can be visited without any pious intention. So they really are a very strange phenomenon in the place where they are. Why do we not find them in the old town halls of, e.g., Nuremberg or Muenster?

The answer is to be found in the implicitly accepted cosmological outlook of the Middle Ages which was very closely intertwined with the theological and philosophical system of the time. The macrocosmos-microcosmos relationship was not an abstraction, but a very concrete kind of experience. And this experience goes as far back as the very early church, for which the concrete world was part of the prayers through which man related to God. In his letter to the Corinthians, written only thirty years after the death of the Apostle Paul, Clement of Rome gives a mostly forgotten example of understanding the universe in its relationship to God:

> The heavens revolve by His arrangement and are subject to Him in peace. Day and night complete the revolution ordained by Him, and neither interferes in the least with the other. Sun and moon and starry choirs, obedient to His arrangement, roll on in harmony, without any deviation, through their appointed orbits. The earth bears fruit ac-

> cording to His will in its proper seasons, and yields the full amount of food required for men and beasts, and all the living things on it, neither wavering nor altering any of His decrees. The unsearchable decisions that govern the abysses and the inscrutable decisions that govern the deeps are maintained by the same decrees. The basis of the boundless sea, firmly built by His creative act for the collecting of the waters, does not burst the barriers set up all around it, and does precisely what has been assigned to it. For He said: Thus far shalt thou come, and thy billows shall be turned to spray within thee. The ocean, impassable for me, and the worlds beyond it are governed by the same decrees of the Master. The seasons—spring, summer, autumn, and winter—make room for one another in peaceful succession. The stations of the winds at the proper time render their service without disturbance. Ever-flowing springs, created for enjoyment and for health, without fail offer to men their life-sustaining breasts. The smallest of the animals meet in peaceful harmony. All these creatures the mighty Creator and Master of the universe ordained to act in peace and concord, thus benefitting the universe, but most abundantly ourselves who have taken refuge under His mercies through our Lord Jesus Christ: to whom be the glory and majesty forever and evermore. Amen.[3]

Though the concretely known universe is thus quite present in the early fathers of the church—cf. Gregory of Nyssa, Ambrose, Basil, John Chrysostom, Maximus the Confessor, and (to a certain extent, at least, even Augustine)—the Middle Ages integrated it much more extensively than they did. The universe present in the Middle Ages refers extensively to Boethius, to the Pseudo-Dionysius Areopagita, to Isidore of Seville, and was most influenced by Plato's Timaeus, to which the discovery of Aristotle—mediated by the Arabs—made only minor corrections.

Essentially, the world was seen as an hierarchical order most perfectly represented by the seven planets which transmitted the movement of the *firmamentum*—which was appropriately separated from the *empyreum* by the *coelum cristallinum*, the upper waters of the Genesis-story of Creation – to the elements which composed the earth. A very short description of this universe is e.g. to be found in Bonaventure's *Breviloquium*:

> Concerning the existence of material nature the following points are to be held: the entire material of the world machine comprises a heavenly and an elementary nature. The heavenly nature is mainly divided into three heavens: the empyrean, the crystalline heaven, and the firmament. Within the firmament (the starry heaven) there are seven planets: Saturn, Jupiter, Mars, the Sun, Venus, Mercury, and the Moon. The elementary nature is divided into four spheres: fire, air, water and earth. From the highest point in heaven to the center of the earth there are in all ten celestial and four elementary spheres. Thus the whole material world machine is constructed in a distinct, perfect and ordered manner.[4]

The intimate knowledge of this universe and its hierarchical structure and functioning was the precondition for being admitted to studies of theology. In the long listings of the theses of the masters of theology of the university of Paris in the 13th century the titles repeat one another to exhaustion on the following line e.g.: Bernard of Trillia: *Quaestiones in spheram Joannis de Sacro Bosco*; Dirk of Freiburg: *De Universitate entium; de animatione caeli, de elementis in quantum sunt partes mundi; de intelligentiis et motoribus caelorum*; Henry of Ghent, *Opus sex dierum*; Peter of Auvergne, *De Caelo et mundo*; Arnold de Villanova: *Compendium astrologiae de juidiciis infirmitatum secundum motum planetarum*; Roger Bacon: *De Cometis; Tractatum de astrorum juidiciis; Naturalis philosophia*; etc.

The universe with its perfectly working machine was thus the essential and implicitly accepted background of medieval thinking in theology. The well-ordered universe receiving all its movement from the empyreum is the ideal background before which the *quinque viae* win a really convincing profile—which they have widely lost before the background of our more or less chaotic universe.

This vision of an ordered universe penetrated not only theological arguments, but the whole life of the Middle Ages. The number seven of the planets—those planets through which all material, natural movement on earth is transmitted finally from the first mover ("*Homo generat hominem et Sol*," otherwise there would be a "mooncalf" since "the inferior bodies are ruled by God by means of the heavenly bodies" [ScG III, 82])—this number seven is the key to understanding all order. Bonaventure found it a mysterious number, which he finds in the "*mundus archetypyus*," and in the order of the earth: There are seven days in a week, and candelabra in the temple had seven branches, the Holy Spirit grants seven gifts, in music, there are seven tones, there are seven pillars of Wisdom (Proverbs 9:1). John writes to the seven churches of Asia and sees Christ appear between seven golden candlesticks. There are seven virtues, four cardinal virtues corresponding to the lower planets and three theological ones corresponding to the upper planets.

The seven sacraments are among the most known parts of the medieval heritage. Even in Trento some cardinals argued for the seven sacraments by referring to the seven planets, and Albert the Great compares the influence of the planets—on which depends all bodily movement which follow the laws of nature—to the influence of God's grace through the seven sacraments in the human soul (*Summa theologica* II XI, q. 53). The sacrament of the "*ordo*" is divided up into four minor and three high consecrations depicting the order of the planets.

In normal non-clerical society the order of the world was as potential ordering factor, as may be seen in the "*libre del ordre de cavayleria*" which begins with the words: "*per significanca de les*

VII planetes." The order of the seven planets is repeated in man himself: as the perfect microcosmos he mirrors the macrocosmos in all its seven parts: The four elements, which compose his body, reflect the lower planets, while the three faculties of the soul – intelligence, memory and will (Bonaventure) – are the counterpart of the three upper planets.

The whole universe is thus ordered in such a way that it reflects the divine wisdom. And this idea of concretely perceived order is not only present in theological manuals of the Middle Ages, but quite evident in preaching and in art. When in prayer the medieval man appealed to the wonders of nature, he did not look to flowers and animals. The most striking example is Francis of Assisi, who is said to have preached to the birds and the wild beasts; but in his Hymn to the Sun, which praises God thanking Him for all Creatures, the sun, the moon, the stars and the four elements are named, but no animal is mentioned. They are, in medieval view, the same as fire, air, water and earth.

Preaching referred often to the planets and the stars. The sermon of magister Guiardus, which compares monks to the stars, is quite revealing:

> *Stella non movetur moto proprio sed sequitur motum firmamenti, sic et veri claustrales non debent moveri propria voluntate sed motu firmamenti, scilicet Dei. Sed multi motu contrario moventur, sequentes proprias voluntates, et proter hoc dicit Daniel (8:10) 'Cornu arietis dejecit de stellis et conculcavit eos'. . . Stella . . . in uno loco fixa est, sic religiosi et clerici fixi debent esse ut loca sua non mutent. . . Sed quidam sunt qui contrarium faciunt.*[5]

Since the whole *machina mundi* as the work of an infinitely wise God could not run in vain, the world must have a purpose. This was found in the need of God to restore the original order which was disturbed by the fall of the angels. Most medieval theologians thought that man was only created as a substitute for the fallen angels, while a few took a more generous approach, ascribing to man an unconditioned creative act in God. In any case, this universe was to come to its end, whenever the number of fallen angels had been made up for by saints or by virgins only (cf. Hugo Ripelin, *Compendium theologiae veritatis*, II, 24). By the time this number is reached, the whole *machina universi* will come to a standstill.[6]

If after this short review we now turn back to that astronomical clock in the cathedral, we see it an image of the universe as it was integrated into the medieval theology. And it might be worthwhile to reflect on the loss of concreteness in prayers like the "Lord's prayer," where the medieval man had only to look at the sky—or in technically more advanced times at the astronomical clock—to see how His "will is done in the heavens" and to strive for the fulfillment of God's will one earth.

But not only in prayers does this world vision of the Middle Ages come through. There is no way to understand Shakespeare without this background. A quote from *Troilus and Cressida* (I,3) might give some indication:

> The heavens themselves, the planets, and this center
> Observe degree, priority, and place,
> Insisture, course, proportion, season, form,
> Office, and custom, in all line of order;
> And therefore is the glorious planet Sol
> In noble eminence enthron'd and spher'd
> Amidst the other; whose medi'cinable eye
> Corrects the ill aspects of planets evil
> And posts, like the commandment of a king,
> Sans check to good and bad. But when the planets
> In evil mixture to disorder wander,
> What plagues and what portents, what mutiny.
> What raging of the sea, shaking of the earth,
> Commotion in the winds, frights changes horrors,
> Divert and crack, rend and deracinate
> The unity and married calm of states
> Quite from their fixture. Oh when degree is shak'd

Which is the ladder to all high designs,
The enterprise is sick. How could communities,
Degree in schools and brotherhoods in cities,
Peaceful commerce from dividable shores,
The primogenitive and due of birth,
Prerogative of age, crowns, scepters, laurels,
But by degree stand in authentic place?
Take but degree away, untune that string,
And hark, what discord follows. Each thing meets
In mere oppugnancy. The bound waters
Should lift their bosoms higher than the shores
And make a sop of all this solid globe:
Thrength should be lord to imbecility,
And the rude son should strike his father dead...
This chaos, when degree is suffocate,
Follows the choking.

In MacBeth, the witches on the heath overturning the value-system—"Right is wrong and wrong is right"—precede the scene where strange signs in heavens and on earth are told.

Only with this background of a perfectly understood and philosophically and theologically integrated *machina mundi* can the shocking effect of the Copernican and Galilean hypothesis be really understood—and perhaps as well the disappointed flight of modern man to subjectivism.

Notes:

[1]Alfred North Whitehead: *Adventures of Ideas*, Cambridge University Press, 1961, p. 19.

[2]Hortus Deliciarum II, Editions du Mont Ste. Odile, 1984, planche 1.

[3]Clement of Rome, I. Corinthians 20, *The Epistles of St. Clement of Rome and of St. Ignatius of Antioch*; translated and annotated by James A. Kleist in *Ancient Christian Writers*, I.

[4]*Breviloquium*, p. II, c. III, no. 1; cf. II Sent., d.2,II,a.1.q.1,d.14, p.I, q.1 and p. II, a.1, q.3.

[5]quoted from M. M. Davy, *Les sermons universitaires parisiens de 1250-1251, Etudes de Philosophie médiévale 15* Paris 1931, 231-37, (Just as a star does not move by its own motion but follows the movement of the firmament, so true monks ought not to move by their own will but by the motion of the firmament, namely God.... But many, following their own will, move by a contrary motion, and for this reason Daniel says, 'The horn of the Ram ejects them from the heavens and tramples upon them.' (8:10) ....Just as a star is fixed in one place, so too religious and clerics ought to be fixed in order that they do not change place.... Yet there are those who do the opposite...).

[6]cf. Th. Aq., *Comp. Theol.*, cap. 171: *Est igitur ultimus finis motus caeli multiplicatio hominum producendorum ad vitam aeternam.... Completo igitur numero hominum ad vitam aeternam producendorum, et eis in vita aeterna contitutis, motus caeli cassabit.*

For more information and literature see:

N. Max Wildiers, *The theologian and his universe – Theology and Cosmology from the Middle Ages to the Present*, The Seabury Press, New York, 1982. (For more complete quotations from the medieval texts use the original Dutch version – quotations in Latin: *Wereldbeeld en Teologie van de Middeleeuwen tot vandaag*, Antwerpen 1977 – or the German version: *Weltbild und Theologie*, Benziger Verlag, Einsiedeln & Zurich.)

Part Two

Curriculum Papers

Workshop on Modern Thought

Frederick Ferré
Workshop Leader

Workshop Leader's Introduction

Frederick Ferré

The participants in the Workshop on Modern Thought decided to distribute their efforts along the formative time span ranging from the late Renaissance into the nineteenth century. They tried to think of themselves as designing a mammoth (probably impossible) course on "Nature and God in Modern Thought," thinking through the overall shape of any such "course" as a whole before dividing it into units for bibliographical detail.

The consensus was that the period from the sixteenth to the nineteenth century could be treated in some ways like a drama. The curtain rises with the sense of a new age dawning. John Hittinger's selections from Machiavelli to Leibniz ring changes on that theme. Whatever the differences between the founders of the modern way of thinking, especially on issues relating nature and God, there was no tendency toward continuing medieval business as usual. Radical change was in the air. One of the key difficulties raised by such new ways of conceiving of nature was understanding how ideas of purpose, or final causation, could remain part of the natural order at all, as James Salmon shows with his annotated bibliography running from Galileo through Boyle and Newton. But the early action of this modern drama, as Wesley Henry's selections illustrate, exudes confidence that the new concepts of nature could lead though natural theology to a secure affirmation of God, as designer and energizer of the world. Goethe, attempting to bring science and religion together in his work, as Walter Gulick shows, was in many ways a climactic exemplar of such confidence. But Gulick's next section, on Kant, marks another sort of climax and turning point in the drama: an immense intellectual challenge to the theoretical possibility of any such unities between the world of nature and reason, on the one hand, and the domain of God and faith, on the other.

After Kant it could be seen that three main alternatives remained for modern approaches to nature and God: existentialist "leaps" in one direction or another, as illustrated in William Garland's bibliographies of Kierkegaard, Nietzsche, and Dostoevsky; continued reliance on systematic rational construction, as attempted in Hegel's monumental reply to Kant, through which Stanley Riukas provides a guide; or frank skepticism, in the tradition from Hume to Mach laid out by Donald Jarnevic and Donald Olive.

Given this situation, one might well expect the modern drama to close lustily, as with the case studies in controversy developed by Joseph Colombo: the first one thundering out of the crucial struggles between geological science and religious belief and the second echoing in the halls of theology over attempts by Schleiermacher and others to accommodate religion to science through theological modernism. Our curtain comes down on the noisiest controversy of them all, the challenge of Darwinism to concepts of God as providential creator, as annotated by Edward Schoen. After that we are no longer simply moderns; we have entered the contemporary world.

The members of the Workshop on Modern Thought were quite aware that a "course" of this size, probably requiring at least two years, could probably never be launched within the constraints of educational reality. But their hope was that the individual modules could be seen in their respective contexts, contributing not only to less comprehensive efforts – e.g. topical courses like ones on science and religion – but also to a larger picture of the shifting relationships between concepts of nature and God.

Six

Concepts of Nature and God in Early Modern Philosophy

John P. Hittinger

Niccolo Machiavelli (1469-1527)

The Prince. Translated with an introduction by Leo Paul S. DeAlvarez. Irving Texas: University of Dallas, 1980.

Chapter 15: criticism of "principalities of the imagination" (e.g., Plato and Augustine); recommendation to study men as they *are* and not as they *ought* to be; this is called an "effective truth."

Chapter 30: discussion of the role of fortune in human affairs and the various responses to it; recommends the bold and fierce attempt to dominate and conquer chance and fortune, treating her like "a woman" to be knocked down.

Francis Bacon (1561-1626)

The Works of Francis Bacon. collected and edited by James Spedding, Robert L. Ellis, and Douglas Heath. originally published in 1870. reprinted by Garret Press, New York New York.

Of the Proficience and Advancement of Learning, Divine and Human, part II on the division of the sciences. (Vol. 4)

One finds here an attempt to eliminate natural theology from the realm of legitimate study. "By undermining its methodological position, he could nullify the influence of this discipline without ever engaging in a pitched battle over particular issues." Collins, *God in Modern Philosophy*, p. 91. He makes metaphysics a part of physics and leaves theology insulated from nature and reason.

"Of Principles and Origins" and "Of True Wisdom." (Vol. 4)

Matter is seen as self-sufficient. Divine causality is strictly a matter of faith.

Essays. "Of Atheism" (16). (Vol. 4)

Claims that science leads to religion, not atheism. But it does this through emotion and faith, not reason.

New Organon see especially the Great Instauration, and Aphorisms part I. (Vol. 4)

The shift from a speculative science to a practical science is noteworthy; the idols of the mind serve a similar function to Descartes' doubt; the attack on final causes is important; finally do we have a re-reading of the Eden myth at the end of part I?

Thomas Hobbes (1588-1679)

Leviathan. Edited by Michael Oakeshott. Oxford, Blackwell, 1946.

Part I:

Chapters xi and xii - In his account of religion, Hobbes traces belief back to curiosity and fear of the world. The desire to control the forces or nature, or at least to appease them, is the origin of science and religion. We only know our own feelings of awe and fear at the power in the universe. "The whole of natural theology is thus reduced to as system of emotive names contrived by man to piece out his ignorance and terror before the power of the universe." Collins, *God in Modern Philosophy*, p. 96

Part II:

Chapter 31 - "the kingdom of God in nature" contains a discussion of the divine attributes.

Chapter 34 - the signification of spiritual terms.

René Descartes (1596-1650)

The Philosophical Works of Descartes. Translated by E. S. Haldane and G. R. Ross. Revised edition. 2 vols. Cambridge, the University Press, 1967.

Discourse on Method. (Vol. 1)

Part I: on the Jesuit education and the role of theology; criteria of certitude and utility are used to criticize received education; does he use the Baconian ruse to get rid of theology by elevating it beyond his poor limited mind?

Part II: the praise of rational unity in human constructions, including the Spartan state; this reveals an instrumental view of reason.

Part III: provisional guide for action; until possibilities of conquest are discovered.

part IV: short sketch of his metaphysics - the cogito and the proof for God.

part V: a likely story - the derivation of the world from mechanical principles; no need for soul to account for life.

Part VI: on the new aim of science: to become "masters and owners of nature", thus prolonging life and producing an "infinity of devices" to make life more convenient.

Meditations. (Vol. 1)

I: statement of hyperbolic doubt.

II: self as thinking thing

III: proof for God

V: restatement of proof, and transition to world

"The three proofs start from the idea of the infinite, the mind having this idea and the idea of a supremely perfect being. The first two proofs are a posteriori, aiming to show that the mind and its idea of the infinite are effects demanding the existence of an infinite cause. The third one is a priori, based on the inherent, rational necessities in the true idea of God as the supremely perfect being." Collins, *God in Modern Philosophy*, p. 60.

Replies Second Set of Objections and Replies. (Vol. 2)
Note objections raised by Thomas Hobbes.

Arguments that Demonstrate the Existence of God. Summary of various arguments for God's existence. (Vol. 2)

Blaise Pascal (1623-1662)

Pensees (and) *Provincial Letters*. Translated by W. F. Trotter and Thomas McCrie, New York, Modern Library, 1941.

10, 12: on the futility of metaphysical proofs for God's existence

210b, 246, 247, 514: on the hidden God

43, 210b, 311, 316: the human condition

223: the "wager" argument

An interesting apologetic in the face of skepticism and the new mechanism.

Benedict Spinoza (1632-1677)

The Collected Works of Spinoza Edited and translated by Edwin Curley. Princeton, Princeton University Press, 1985. Vol. 1.

"Short Treatise on God, Man, and His Well Being." A brief treatment of the problem of God, also in geometrical fashion.

Ethics Part I: on God. see especially definitions and axioms, and Propositions I, XIV, XV, XVI XXIX, XXXIII, and the appendix containing arguments against final causality.

"*Deus sive nature*" God or nature, the two are identical; thus we have the classic statement and argument for pantheism.

Tractatus Theologico-Politicus. First sketch of higher biblical criticism.

The Cambridge Platonists

The Cambridge Platonists. Edited by Gerald R. Craig. New York, Oxford University Press, 1968. Reprinted by University Press of America.

Nathanael Culverwell, "An Elegant and Learned Discourse of the Light of Nature."

Henry More, "An Antidote Against Atheism."

Ralph Cudworth, "On the Indefensible Arguments of the Atheists."

Arguments for the existence of God and the soul aimed primarily against Hobbes.

John Locke (1632-1704)

Two Treatises of Government. Edited by Peter Laslett. Cambridge, Cambridge University Press, 1970.

"Second Treatise," sections 4 and 6. On man as the "workmanship" of God.

"First Treatise," interpretation of the Old Testament against the divine right of kings.

Essay Concerning Human Understanding. Edited by Peter Nidditch. Oxford University Press, 1980.

I.4.7-17 On God as an innate idea.

II.21.70-73 A variation of Pascal's wager argument.

IV.10.all A proof for the existence of God.

IV.18.all On faith and reason

IV.19.all On religious enthusiasm.

Reasonableness of Christianity. Edited with introduction by George W. Ewing. Chicago, Gateway Edition, 1965.

Reasonableness of Christianity: With a Discourse on Miracles and A Third Letter Concerning Toleration. Edited, abridged and introduced by I. T. Ramsey. Stanford, Stanford University Press, 1958. George

Discussion of the role of Christianity in moral and political life.

Nicholas Malebranche (1638-1715)

Dialogues on Metaphysics and on Religion. Translated by M. Ginsberg. London, Allen and Unwin, 1923.

The Search After Truth. Translated by Thomas M. Lennon and Paul J. Olscamp. Columbus, Ohio State University, 1980.

See especially Book III, part 2, c. 6 "We see all things in God."

The three main teachings are: "occasionalism, or the sole causality of God; the intuitive vision of God; and the vision of other things in God." Collins, p. 86.

G. W. Leibniz (1646-1716)

New Essays on Human Understanding. Translated and edited by Peter Remnant and Jonathan Bennett. Cambridge, Cambridge University Press, 181.

Book I, On innate ideas

Book IV.10, On the existence of God

Very pointed criticisms of Locke's *Essay.*

Leibniz Selections. Translated by P. Wiener. New York, Scribner, 1951.

Monadology

Principles of Nature and Grace

On the Ultimate Origins of Things

Discourse on Metaphysics

Theodicy: Essays on the Goodness of God, the Freedom of Man, and the Origin of Evil. Edited with an introduction by Austin Farrer. Translated by E. M. Huggard. La Salle, Illinois, Open Court, 1965.

Discussion of order in the universe and man's place in it.

Seven

Final Cause in Early Modern Philosophy

James Salmon, S.J.

Galileo Galilei (1564-1642)

A. Primary Works:

Dialogues and Mathematical Demonstrations Concerning Two New Sciences, trans. by Stillman Drake, University of Wisconsin Press, 1974.

> Editor's preface: "To give us the science of motion God and Nature have joined hands and created the intellect of Galileo" (Fra Paolo Sarpi).

Letter to the Grand Duchess Christina, trans. by S. Drake, Doubleday Anchor Books, 1957.

> ". . .in the discussion of natural problems, we ought not to begin at the authority of places in scripture, but at the sensible experiments and necessary demonstrations. For, from the Divine Word, the sacred scripture and nature did both alike proceed . . . Nature, being inexorable and immutable, and never passing the bounds of the laws assigned her . . . I conceive that concerning natural effects, that which either sensible experience sets before our eyes, or necessary demonstrations do prove unto us, ought not, upon any

account, to be called into question, much less condemned upon the testimony of texts of scripture, which may, under theory words, couch senses seemingly contrary thereto . . . Nor does God less admirably discover himself to us in Nature's actions, than in Scripture's sacred dictions" (pp. 182-3).

Dialogue Concerning the Two Chief World Systems, trans. by S. Drake, Univ. of California Press, 1967.

Salv. ". . . if he will but assure me, who is the mover of one of these movables (Mars and Jupiter), I will undertake to be able to tell him who makes the earth to move. Nay, more; I will undertake to be able to do the same if he can but tell me, who moves the parts of the earth downwards."

Simp. "The cause of this is most manifest, and every one knows that it is gravity."

Salv. ". . .you should say that everyone knows that it is called gravity; but I do not question you about the name, but about the essence of the thing . . . not as if we really understood anymore, what principle or virtue that is, which moves a stone downwards, than we know who moves it upwards, when it is separated from the projicient, or who moves the moon round, except only the name, which more particularly and properly we have assigned to all motion of descent, namely gravity" (p. 210).

B. Secondary Works:

E. A. Burtt, *The Metaphysical Foundations of Modern Physical Science*, Routledge and Kegan Paul, London, 1932.

Ch. III for discussion of local motion, Galileo's method, primary and secondary qualities, God and the physical world.

E. J. Dyksterhuis, *The Mechanization of the World Picture*, Princeton, 1986.

Pages 333-359 for an excellent description (for general reader) of contributions by Galileo to the science of mechanics, integrating the Dialogues with discussion of his theses.

W. Wallace, *Galileo and His Sources: The Heritage of the Collegio Romano in Galileo's Science*, Princeton, 1984.

In the Preface Wallace notes "These results (Galileo's notebooks) obviously have profound implications for anyone interested in the origins of the Scientific Revolution, and particularly in the continuity between late medieval or scholastic science and that of the early seventeenth century.

Johannes Kepler (1571-1630)

A. Primary Works:

Mysterium Cosmographicum, trans. by A. Duncan, Abaris Books, 1981.

"But after all, why were the distinctions between curved and straight, and the nobility of a curve, among God's intentions when he displayed the universe? Why indeed? Unless because by a most perfect Creator it was absolutely necessary that a most beautiful work should be produced. For it neither is nor was right (as Cicero in his book on the universe quotes from Plato's Timaeus) that he who is the best should make anything except the most beautiful" (Beginning of Chapter II).

Opera Omnia, ed. C. Frisch, Erlangen, 1858 ff.

"*Amat illa* (Nature) *unitatem,*" "*Natura simplicitatem amat.*" "*Numquam in ipsa quicquam otiosum aut superfluum existit.*" "*Natura semper quod potest per faciliora, non agit per ambages difficiles*" (p. 112 vol. I, N.B. early adoption of Copernicanism). Kepler joined Tycho Brahe a year before Brahe's death and attempted to penetrate and understand the meaning of Brahe's data for "fuller knowledge of God through nature and the glorification of his profession" (p. 688, vol. VIII).

Kepler's genuine empirical approach to nature: "without proper experiments I conclude nothing" (p. 224, Vol. V).

Importance of Mathematics: "There are, in fact, as I began to say above, not a few principles which are the special property of mathematics, such principles as are discovered by the common light of nature, require no demonstration and which concern quantities primarily; then they are applied to other things, so far as the latter have something in common with quantities. Now there are more of these principles in mathematics than in the other theoretical sciences because of that very characteristic of the human understanding which seems to be such from the law of creation, that nothing can be known completely except quantities or by quantities. And so it happens that the conclusions of mathematics are most certain and indubitable" (p. 148, vol. VIII). Burtt notes, p. 53, that Kepler reached a new conception of causality, a reinterpretation of formal cause in terms of exact mathematics.

B. Secondary Works:

H. Butterfield, *The Origins of Modern Science*, The Free Press, 1965.

Pages 74-77 for Kepler as mathematician.

E. A. Burtt, *The Metaphysical Foundations of Modern Physical Science*, Routledge and Kegan Paul, London, 1932.

Pages 52-60 for Kepler's new metaphysics.

Pierre Gassendi (1592-1655)

A. Primary Works:

Opera Omneo, Stuttgart-Bad Canstatt, Frommann, 1961.

Animadiversiones in decimum librium Diogenis (The fabric of science based on the hypothesis of atoms founded by Epicurus), trans. by W. Charleton, Johnson Reprint Corp., NY, 1966.

Institutio Logica (1658), Latin and English trans. by H. Jones, Van Gorcum, Assen, The Netherlands, 1981.

"If there is an effect there must be or have been a cause: for example, if it is day, the sun must be shining, if there is a building there must have been a builder" (Canon XVI, Part 2).

The Selected Works of Pierre Gassendi, trans. by C. Bush, Johnson Reprint Corp., NY, 1972.

B. Secondary Works:

H. Egan, *Gassendi's View of Knowledge*, University Press of America, 1984.

This is the best reference found on Gassendi. Gassendi seems to have been an Epicurean atomist who still held for final causality especially in biology and demonstrating the existence of God and his presence in creation. In his inaugural lecture with the chair in mathematics at the Royal College of France he manifests the complexity of his thought. "*Videri potest non incongrue intelligi Deum exercere geometriam, tam dum contemplatur ac potissimum sese ipsum considerat; quam dum agit, maxime vero mundum creat ac moderatur.*" (*Opera Omnia* IV p. 67a) Therefore he used mathematical analogies when speaking of God, comparing God to a sphere whose center is everywhere and whose circumference is nowhere.

F. Copleston, S. J., *A History of Philosophy*, Volume III, Newman, 1960.

Pages 263-4 for a good introduction. He concludes "... his philosophy considered in itself, is a curious amalgam of Epicurean materialism with spiritualism and theism and of a rather crude empiricism with rationalism."

IV. René Descartes (1596-1650)

A. Primary Works:

Oeuvres philosophiques de Descartes, ed. by F. Aliquie, Garnier, Paris 1963-67.

"Know that by nature I do not understand some goddess or some other sort of imaginary power. I employ this word to signify matter itself insofar as I consider it with all the qualities which I have attributed to it, taken together, and under this condition that God continues to conserve it in the same way that he has created it. For solely from the fact that he continues thus to conserve it, it follows with necessity that it (matter thus quantified) must have several changings of its parts, which (changings) not being able (it seems to me) to be properly attributed to God's action, since the latter does not change, I attribute them to nature. And the rules according to which these changings are made, I call the laws of nature." (p. 349, vol. I, translation in J. Collins)

B. Secondary Works:

J. Collins, *Descartes Philosophy of Nature*, American Philosophical Quarterly Monograph Series, Oxford, 1971.

For Descartes considerations on finality see pp. 87-93.

F. Copleston, S. J. *A History of Philosophy*, *op. cit.*.

Volume III explains well how Descartes excluded final causality from natural philosophy or physics.

Robert Boyle (1627-1691)

A. Primary Works:

The Works of the Honourable Robert Boyle, ed. Thomas Birch, 6 volumes, London, 1672.

A compilation of Boyle's works.

The Sceptical Chymist, Dent, London, 1964.

The best known but not the best work.

There are a number of interpretations of Boyle's natural philosophy. In "A True Inquiry into the Vulgarly Received Notion of Nature" (1686) he described the scholastic Aristotelian view of nature that detracts "from the honor of the great author and governor of the world, that men should ascribe most of the admirable things that are to be met within it, not to him, but to a certain nature. . . ." Believing that a sharp distinction between creator and creature is fundamental to Christian faith, he says of this view that it "seems not to me very suitable to the profound reverence we owe the divine majesty since it seems to make the Creator differ too little by far from a created (not to say imaginary) Being." Thus many have felt him close to Descartes.

However, in many of his works Boyle argues against Cartesianism (and the Epicureans) by defending the power of teleological inferences. For example in "A Disquisition about the Final Causes of Natural Things" (1688) he concedes that earth, stones and various metals (inanimate objects) "do not infer any knowledge or intention in their causes." But he goes on: "There are others that require such a number and concourse of conspiring causes, and such a continued series of motions or operations, that it is utterly improbable that they should be produced without the superintendency of a rational agent . . . . And therefore it will not follow, that if chance could produce a slight contexture in a few parts of matter, we may safely conclude it able to produce so exquisite and admirable a contrivance as the body of an animal." Boyle's arguments for teleology are based on both complexity and adaptation independent of efficient causal networks, to generate organisms. His careful distinction between efficient and final causality in the "Disquisition" allows him to be classified as a 17th century mechanist but at the same time to be a defender of teleology in nature in special cases. Further discussion of his attitude towards nature can be found in his essay "The Christian Virtuoso" and "A Free Inquiry. . ."

The Sceptical Chymist, first appearing in 1662, concerns a dialogue between Eleutherius and Carneades (Boyle himself). Eleutherius represents contemporary physicists, who resolved matter into the four elements – earth, air, fire, water – and contemporary chemists who maintained nature was resolvable into three principles – salt, sulfur, mercury. It is in this work that Boyle defined elements a hundred years before Joseph Priestly. He writes: "And to prevent mistakes I must advertise you, that I now mean by elements, as those chymists that speak plainest do by their principles, certain primitive and simple, or perfectly unmingled bodies; which not being made for any other bodies or of one another, are the ingredients of which all those perfectly mixt bodies are compounded, and into which they are ultimately resolved."

B. Secondary Works:

R. Westfall, *Science and Religion in Seventeenth Century England*, Yale, 1958.

T. Kuhn, "Robert Boyle and Structural Chemistry," *Isis* 42 (1952).

Pages 12- 36 for a classic discussion of Boyle's non mathematical atomism.

J. Lennox, "Robert Boyle's Defense of Teleological Inference in Experimental Science," *Isis* 74 (1983) p. 38-52.

F. Copleston, S. J., vol. V, p. 143-7.

Key points:

a) Boyle stressed experimental research before making confident assertions of hypotheses.

b) Respected mathematical structure of nature proposed by Galileo and Descartes as a system of bodies in motion. Motion is not an inherent quality of matter. It is super-added by God, as are the laws of motion.

c) How events occur is not explained by chemists and physicists in terms of final causality.

d) Final causality is relevant to metaphysical explanations. Mechanical interpretations of nature are only adequate within restricted fields (opposing Descartes and Hobbes).

e) Rejected developing tendency to make man a mere spectator of nature.

f) Experimental science is a service of God (Boyle lectures).

g) Believed in divine conservation and concurrence without any systematic harmonization with laws of nature.

Isaac Newton (1642-1727)

A. Primary Works:

Principia Mathematica Philosophiae Naturalis, trans. by A. Motte, University of California Press, 1934.

The General Scholium at the conclusion of Book III is too long to include. Newton writes "This Being governs all things, not as the soul of the world, but as Lord over all." He goes on to describe his understanding of God which is a point of reference in the history of science/religion.

Opticks: or a Treatise of the Reflections, Refractions, Inflections, and Colours of Light, 3rd ed. London, 1721.

"The main business of natural philosophy is to argue from phenomena without feigning hypotheses, and to deduce causes from effects, till we come to the very first cause, which certainly is not mechanical, and not only to unfold the mechanism of the world, but chiefly to resolve these and such like questions. What is there in places almost empty of matter, and whence is it that the sun and planets gravitate towards one another, without dense matter between them? Whence is it that nature doth nothing in vain, and whence arises all that order and beauty which we see in the world? To what end are comets, and whence is it that planets move all one and the same way in orbs concentric, while comets move all manners of ways in orbs very eccentric, and what hinders the fixed start from falling upon one another? How came the bodies of animals to be contrived with so much art, and for what ends were their several parts? Was the eye contrived without skill in optics or the ear without knowledge of sounds? How do motions of the body follow from the will and whence is the instinct of animals? Is not the sensory of animals that place to which the sensitive substance is present, and into which the sensible species of things are carried through the nerves and brain that there they may be perceived by their immediate presence to that substance? And these things being rightly dispatched, does it not appear from phenomena that there is a being incorporeal, living, intelligent, omnipresent, who, in infinite space as it were, in his sensory, sees the things themselves intimately, and thoroughly perceives them; and comprehends them wholly by their immediate presence to himself? . . . And though every true step made in this philosophy brings us not immediately to the knowledge of the first cause, yet it brings us nearer to it, and on that account is to be highly valued." (Opticks Q28, Book 3, Part 1)

Opera Omnia

See especially first letter to Dr. Bentley on occasion of Dr. Bentley's tenure of the Boyle lectureship (1692).

B. Secondary Works:

R. S. Westfall, "The Rise of Science and the Decline of Orthodox Christianity: A Study of Kepler, Descartes, and Newton, in *God and Nature*, ed. by D. Lindberg and R. Numbers, University of California Press, 1986, esp. p. 228-234.

E. Burtt, *The Metaphysical Foundations of Modern Physical Science*, Routledge and Kegan Paul, London 1932,

Chapter VII gives a dated but still valuable systematic discussion of Newton's metaphysics.

I. B. Cohen, "Isaac Newton's *Principia*, the scriptures and the divine providence," pp. 523-48 of S. Morgenbesser, P. Suppes, M. White, ed., *Essays in honor of Ernest Nagel: Philosophy, Science and Method*, St. Martin's NY, 1969.

Often it is said that God appears in the *Principia* only in the second edition (1713) in the concluding Scholium Generale. Cohen shows here that in the first edition (1687) there is a reference to God and divine providence, removed in the second edition. It is interesting to review the great care Newton took with the latter to add then this General Scholium in the second edition – which involves correspondence with Cotes and Bentley.

Eight

Classic Modern Natural Theologies

Wesley L. Henry

John Ray (1627-1705)

Ray, John. *Wisdom of God in the Creation*. London: Dove, 1827.

The full title of the book is an outline of its contents. That title reads: *The Wisdom of God Manifested in the works of the Creation: In Two Parts; viz. The heavenly Bodies, Elements, Meteors, Fossils, Vegetables, Animals, (Beasts, Birds, Fishes, and Insects) more particularly in the Body of the Earth, its Figure, Motion, and Consistency, and in the admirable Structure of the Bodies of Man, and other Animals, as also in their Generations, etc. With Answers to some Objections*. There is repeated citing of scientific descriptions of organisms which show evidence of design, but this evidence is not put into a formal argument for the existence of a creator or designer. Ray wrote as though it ought to be obvious from the intricacies of organisms described by science that they must be the result of intelligent planning.

Ray rejects the concept of a world composed of atoms in motion or matter in motion in favor of an innate organising principle in the organic world. This vitalistic principle becomes a type of intermediary through which God works in the creation. For Ray this helps him explain why the generation of things is a slow and gradual process, and why there are some peculiarities and malformations to be found in nature. The latter, however, are turned into positive evidence for God's existence rather than evidence against. Thus, the book generally contains evidence of contrivances and purposive relationships in the context of a design argument.

Ray, John. *The Correspondence of John Ray.* Edited by Edwin Lankester. London 1848.

The letters cited are mostly on botanical subjects and of little use in the 20th century. However, there are some points made from time to time in the letters which are germane to the discussion of nature and God. The following example comes from page 154.

> Were these bodies produced by a concretion of salts, it seems strange to me that there would be such great variety of them, and their shapes so regular and exactly circumscribed; so great a diversity of figures arguing a greater variety of salts, or of the modifications and mixtures of salts, than are likely to be found in nature; and the curvilineous concretions of slats never, that I have yet seen, appearing in that regularity of figure and due circumscription as in these bodies, which is an argument that the government of some principle superior to matter figured and moved in their formation.

Goodman, D. C. *Science and Religious Belief 1600-1900* The Open University Press 1973.

This book is part of the Open University course on "New Interactions between Theology and Natural Science" and is a source book of primary readings. Chapters 11 and 12 are selections from Ray's *Wisdom of God* and *Three Physico-Theological Discourses*.

Nebelsick, Harold. *Theology and Science in Mutual Modification*. New York: Oxford University Press, 1981.

Although covering a period of history much beyond the 17th and 18th centuries, there is a brief discussion of Ray in the *initial chapter* in the midst of talking about other persons of his time who related God and nature.

Raven, Charles E. *John Ray, Naturalist*. Cambridge: Cambridge University Press, 1942.

This massive biography of John Ray brings together most everything relevant to comprehending Ray's career and is much too extensive for most uses of Ray. Although most of the book is concerned with Ray's science, the final chapter entitled "The Wisdom of God" is an excellent discussion of Ray's concept of God and nature Indeed, Raven argues that Paley utilized it, even plagiarized it, in his *Natural Theology*.

Westfall, Richard. *Science and Religion in Seventeenth-Century England*. New Haven: Yale University Press, 1958.

There are allusions to Ray scattered throughout this book. Because of the organization of Westfall's book, one cannot point to just one chapter as containing all the needed information. But pages 45-48 and pages 127-130 are especially good. Westfall writes, "The number of the Lord's works, beyond the power of man to investigate, demonstrates the extent of the Creator's skill and the wealth of His power and wisdom. . . . On the earth alone dwell at least a hundred and fifty species of beasts, some five hundred species of birds, perhaps three thousand fish, twenty thousand insects, and more plants. I the number of creatures be so exceeding great, how immense must be the power and wisdom of Him Who made them?" This citation is taken to represent Ray's line of thought.

(Two additional men who probably ought to be considered because they fit into this period are John Wilkins (1614-1672) who wrote *Of the Principles and Duties of Natural Religion* and William Derham (1657-1735) who wrote *Physico-Theology: or a Demonstration of the Being and Attributes of God, from His Works of Creation* Both men have selections in the D. C. Goodman book cited above.)

John Toland (1670-1722)

Toland, John. *Christianity not Mysterious: or a Treatise Shewing, that There is Nothing in the Gospel Contrary to Reason, nor above it: And that No Christian Doctrine can be properly call'd a Mystery.* London 1696.

In the preface, he states his basic assertion: "The true Christian can no more be offended when he finds one employ Reason, not to enervate or perplex, but to confirm and elucidate Revelation." p. vii. The book is designed to prove Toland's fundamental belief that God is the designer of the universe, the original mechanic who constructed it. After arguing that point, he then goes on to argue that such a God is worthy of worship. Section III, chapter 2 is especially pertinent for a discussion of the concept of God and the attending properties. Toland argues the belief, "As for God, we comprehend nothing better than his attributes."

Gay, Peter. *Deism: an Anthology.* Princeton: D. Van Nostrand Co., 1968.

This book has an informative introduction to the deist environment in chapters one and two, and then there are readings taken from key English, Continental, and American thinkers, including a selection from Toland's Christianity Not Mysterious."

Daniel, Stephen H. *John Toland, his Methods, Manners, and Mind.* Montreal: McGill-Queen's University Press, 1984.

This book is a treatment of the complete works of John Toland. One should see particularly the introductory chapter for help in placing Toland in the stream of thought on science and religion. Chapter two for Toland's understanding of reason and how it is suited to religious topics is also quite good. At the end of the book, there is a what seems to be a complete bibliography of works by Toland and a listing of secondary sources which relate to the period.

Nebelsick, Harold. *Theology and Science in Mutual Modification*

This book cited earlier also makes reference to Toland at several places.

Sullivan, Robert E. *John Toland and the Deist Controversy*

Samuel Clarke (1675-1729)

Clarke, Samuel. *Demonstration of the Being and Attributes of God (Boyle Lectures 1704*). London 1711

Clarke, Samuel. *A Discourse Concerning the Unchangeable Obligations of Natural Religion and the Truth and Certainty of the Christian Revelation (Boyle Lectures 1705).* London 1711.

Clarke gives what he calls an *a priori* proof for God's existence in the first part of his book *Demonstration of the being and Attributes of God.* The proof moves from asserting that every being is either a dependent being or an independent being, to either there exists an independent being or every being is dependent, to asserting that it is false that every being is dependent, to asserting the existence of an independent being, which Clarke then argues must be a necessary being. In the process of stating the argument, he explains what he means by necessary being. The discussion by Clarke of the terms in his argument raises some of the issues which have been discussed in the literature since then. After the first 45 pages or so, there follows a discussion of the attributes of God. A current writer, William L. Rowe, has also attempted to explicate Clarke's concept of God and would be of help in understanding this book.

Clarke, Samuel. *The Leibniz-Clarke Correspondence*. Edited by H. G. Alexander. New York: Barnes and Noble, 1956.

The introduction on pages xiii-xviii has a good summary statement on the point about God and nature discussed by the two men in their correspondence. The first Leibniz letter and first Clarke reply has a discussion of God as an artificer. The second letter contains Clarke's position stated in this way: "God is present to the world, not as a part, but as a governor; acting upon all things, himself acted upon by nothing." Although all of the letters could be used, it seems that the first two are the ones most closely related to the themes of God and nature.

Ferguson, James. *The Philosophy of Dr. Samuel Clarke and Its Critics*. New York: Vantage Press, 1974.

This book has a chapter on the meaning of *a priori* in Clarke's time and what it meant for him. There is also a summary of Clarke's argument for God's existence on pages 22-28, a summary of the Clarke-Leibniz Correspondence, and a wealth of information on Clarke's relationship to other important figures of his time.

Westfall, *Science and Religion in Seventeenth-Century England*.

See the chapter on Divine Providence and natural law for a general discussion of providence and natural law as conceived by Clarke's contemporaries. The chapter also contains a specific discussion of Clarke and Leibniz and their differences on these matters as argued in the correspondence.

Joseph Butler (1692-1752)

Butler, Joseph. *The Analogy of Religion, Natural and Revealed.* London: Macmillan and Co., 1900.

What Butler is concerned to show in the *Analogy* is that the probability of religion (Christianity) is sufficient for it to be sensible to make religion the basis of human action. Butler even has a theory on how great this probability needs to be. There are five doctrines discussed in the book. (1) Immortality of the Soul, (2) God's Rewards and Punishments, (3) Virtue, (4) Life as Probation, (5) God's Moral Government. In the midst of discussing these points, Butler argues in general for a special view of nature which finds an intention behind the regularities of nature and a set of prescriptive laws. The view of the universe as a vast machine is present here. Butler's general argument is characterized by the statement, ". . . to an unprejudiced mind the ten thousand instances of design cannot but prove a designer."

Austin, Duncan-Jones. *Butler's Moral Philosophy.* Baltimore: Penguin Books, 1952.

Chapter one is a good statement about his life and writings. Most of the book is concerned with moral concepts, but chapter seven on the place of God in Butler's ethics would be especially helpful for understanding the themes of God and nature in Butler. It deals with the ideas of final cause, human goodness, and God's love among other topics.

Broad, C. D. *Five Types of Ethical Theory.* London 1930.

The section on Butler is helpful although it is directed towards moral theory rather than theistic concepts.

Harris, William C. *Teleology in the Philosophy of Joseph Butler and Abraham Tucker* Philadelphia: University of Pennsylvania, 1941.

This work is not nearly as extensive as others and is of limited value. The first half of the short book is on Butler and deals with his concepts of the order of nature, the ends of the universe, and teleology and morality. Chapter one especially deals with God and nature in Butler's system.

Mossner, E. C. *Bishop Butler and the Age of Reason.* New York: The Macmillan Company, 1936.

The introduction provides biographical matter which places Butler in a tradition. Chapter three provides an account of Butler's argumentation on the existence and attributes of God. Butler is shown to be content to show the "ways of Providence" are sufficiently probable to satisfy practical faith. A full bibliography is appended after a final chapter of evaluation.

Norton, William J. *Bishop Butler, Moralist & Divine.* New Brunswick: Rutgers University Press, 1940.

Although the book has as its primary purpose the understanding of Butler's views on morality, the author finds himself "piecing together Butler's system of metaphysics" as he says. Part V in the "Nature of the University" discusses the universe as ideal, as spiritual, in relation to God, and man's place in it. Part VI has a section on natural religion.

Penelhum, Terence. *Butler.* London: Routledge and Kegan, 1985.

The primary purpose of the book is to expound Butler's moral concepts. But the author finds himself giving a large portion of his effort to the philosophy of religion. See especially chapter IV on Butler's Apologetics and chapter V on Identity and the Future Life for an analysis of Butler's thought on God and nature, among other matters.

Spooner, W. A. *Bishop Butler.* London: Methuen and Company, 1901.

Chapter one is an informative accounting of Butler's life. Chapters five and six are an explication of Butler's *Analogy*. The chapters are written in great detail and provide a wealth of information on Butler's methodology and conclusions.

Whyte, Alexander. *Bishop Butler, an Appreciation with the Best Passages of his Writings Selected.* London: Oliphant Anderson and Ferrier, 1903.

The lengthy introduction is an openly sympathetic statement on the genius of Butler and how he fits into his age of brilliant contemporaries. What follows is a listing of key passages. The sections on God, the Love of God, Reason, of Means and Ends are especially appropriate to the themes of God and nature.

Jeffner, Anders. *Butler and Hume on Religion.* Stockholm, 1966.

There is a good exposition of Butler's basic views on religion and morality. Chapter three on the general analogy argument is especially very helpful in understanding Butler's basic approach to theistic questions.

William Paley (1743-1805)

Paley, William. *Natural Theology: or, Evidences of the Existence and Attributes of the Deity, collected from the Appearances of Nature*. Philadelphia: John F. Watson, 1814.

______. *Natural Theology*. Edited with introduction by Frederick Ferré. New York: Bobbs-Merrill Company, 1963.

______. *The Principle of Moral and Political Philosophy*. 2 Vols. New York: B and S. Collins, 1835.

______. *Works*. 6 Vols. Cambridge: Hilliard and Brown, 1835.

For purposes of teaching a module on Paley, the Ferré edition provides all the guidance one really needs. The introduction outlines the framework of the argument, and then the text itself supplies the pertinent original sections of Paley's *Natural Theology*

In the *Principles of Moral and Political Philosophy*, the chapters on Human Happiness, Divine Benevolence, and the Moral Sense would be helpful in talking about God's relationship to humanity.

Brougham, Henry Lord. *Dissertations on Subjects of Science Connected with natural Theology*. 2 Vols. London: C. Knight and Co., 1839.

Volume II has a lengthy section on the origin of evil and how the problem affects the divine attributes. See the first eighty pages.

Paxton, James. *Illustration of Paley's Natural Theology*. Boston: Hilliard, Gray, Little, and Wilkins, 1827.

This is a book written to illustrate the contrivances of natural objects Paley utilizes in his *Natural Theology*. The illustrations are correlated to the chapters of *Natural Theology* which make use of organisms having mechanical functions, as bones, muscles, etc. The book has explanatory value when tied directly to Paley's examples. The book illustrates the importance attached to Paley's work in his time.

Stephen, Leslie. *History of English Thought* 2 Vols. London, 1881.

Stephen takes Paley and talks about him in Volume I. Stephen is not so valuable for elucidating Paley's argument as he is for attempting to criticize Paley's argument and assess its long-range importance.

Nine

Goethe on God and Nature

Walter Gulick

Goethe has been ranked with Dante and Shakespeare as one of the European literary greats. Although foremost a poet, Goethe has something of the cast of the Renaissance man. His writings include genres as diverse as dramas, novels, an autobiography, scientific treatises, travel memoirs, fables, essays, and of course poetry. It is difficult to capture the essential Goethe not only because of the span of his concerns but also because his writing style underwent a series of dramatic changes. One would be mistaken to look to Goethe for a calm deliberation on the relationship of science to religion. These topics are but strands in the complex tapestry of his life, and one would be correct in expecting them to intersect only on occasion when guided by the larger patterns in his life.

Goethe – Religious Writings

For Goethe, religion was not the sacrosanct core of his life. In a sense, living his own life passionately and reflectively was his religion. He was filled with respect for Christianity, but he was not personally committed to the church or to any personal devotional life. His personal belief tended toward pantheism, although as with his writings, it is possible to trace various stages in the development of his religious views. His reflections on religious themes are expressed episodically and in epigrams rather than in sustained treatments. The following three works, although differing greatly in style, offer rich treatments of God and religion (sometimes in relation to nature) if one is willing to sift through the text and be an active interpreter of it.

The Autobiography of Johann Wolfgang von Goethe (Dichtung und Wahrheit). Trans. by John Oxenford. 2 vol. Chicago: University of Chicago Press, 1975.

Goethe completed this work shortly before his death, yet it only covers his life up to age 26. While his youthful pietism, iconoclasm and idealism are revealed through the course of the narrative, there are also intimations of his more mature ideas on religion. The autobiography does not reach to the period of Goethe's life when he began his scientific investigations, so science and religion are not thematically discussed in their interrelation.

Goethe's World View: Presented in His Reflections and Maxims. Trans. by Heinz Norden. Edited with an Intro. by Frederick Ungar. New York: Frederick Ungar Publishing Co., 1963.

Ungar's brief introduction highlights Goethe's understanding of God and religion quite effectively. The epigrams and poems included in this work are not specified according to source of date and so are less than ideally helpful if one wished to do a serious study of Goethe's views.

Faust (Parts 1 and 2). Ed. by Walter Arndt. New York: Norton, 1976.

The archetypal work of German literature, this work may be read as involving a conflict between science and religion, the unrelenting search for knowledge versus the need to save one's soul, or in many other ways.

Goethe – Scientific Writings

Goethe's *Schriften zur Naturwissenschaft* runs 20 volumes and includes material in botany, geology, physics, and zoology. It has been estimated that there may be 10,000 additional entries in various languages on Goethe and the sciences. However, the vast majority of the material is more appropriate for a course in the history of science than for one in science and religion. Goethe understood himself to be an amateur in science. Yet he was so dedicated to careful observation that scientists of the status of Heisenberg and Planck have accorded his work great respect. He is credited with discovering the intermaxillary bone in humans, first arguing that the skull developed from the backbone, and founding the science of morphology. His was not a theoretical approach; he emphasized the importance of comprehending the form and function of phenomena through perception. He criticized Newton's *Optics* for reducing light to mathematical terms to the detriment of ordinary experience. Thus Goethe was both active in scientific investigation and critical of the tendency to quantification characteristic of the Enlightenment and the triumph of Newton.

The following two selections include Goethe's most significant scientific work as it bears on religion.

Goethe's Botanical Writings. Trans. by Bertha Mueller. Honolulu: University of Hawaii Press, 1952.

In addition to containing Goethe's "The Metamorphosis of Plants," this book contains a section of Goethe's essays which are most helpful in understanding Goethe's philosophical, scientific, and religious beliefs. Particularly significant are "The Objective and Subjective Reconciled by Means of the Experiment," "Influence of the New Philosophy," "Analysis and Synthesis," and "Nature" (the latter probably written by a follower of Goethe in his spirit).

Goethe's Theory of Colours. Trans. by Charles Lock Eastlake. London: Frank Cass & Company, 1967.

The footnotes indicate how much Goethe's view was influenced by Aristotle and Leonardo da Vinci. This translation is somewhat problematical.

Secondary Sources

Amrine, Frederick, *et. al. Goethe and the Sciences: A Reappraisal*. Dordrecht: D. Reidel Publishing Company, 1987.

This work contains a number of studies on Goethe in the history of science. The titles of two of the essays suggest the focus of much else in the book: "The Theory of Color as the Symbolism of Insight" and "Goethe's Science: An Alternative *to* Modern Science or *within* It – or No Alternative at All?" The book contains a valuable annotated bibliography of books by and about Goethe on science.

Bowman, Derek. *Life into Autobiography: A Study of Goethe's "Dichtung und Wahrheit."* Berne: Herbert Lang, 1971.

Chapter Four deals helpfully with Goethe's views on religion.

Cottrell, Alan P. *Goethe's View of Evil and the Search for a New Image of Man in Our Time*. Edinburgh: Floris Books, 1982.

Through a focus on *Faust*, this work brings scientific, religious, and other cultural disciplines into fruitful juxtaposition.

Gray, Ronald D. *Goethe the Alchemist: A Study of Alchemical Symbolism in Goethe's Literary and Scientific Works*. Cambridge:

Cambridge University Press, 1952 (now available as an AMS reprint).

Gray shows how Goethe was influenced by the mystical aspects of alchemy. He utilized the alchemical tradition to explore for scientific and religious evidence of symbolic truth.

Loewen, Harry. *Goethe's Response to Protestantism*. Berne: Herbert Lang & Co., 1972.

Loewen suggests that Goethe steered a middle course between orthodox Lutheranism and the religious liberalism of his time.

Magnus, Rudolf. *Goethe as a Scientist*. Trans. by Heinz Norden. New York: Henry Schuman, 1949 (German original, 1906).

This work gives a comprehensive overview of Goethe's scientific work. "Goethe's highest joy was to know himself at one with nature in his scientific research" (p. 246).

Nisbet, H. B. *Goethe and the Scientific Tradition*. London: The Institute of Germanic Studies, 1972.

This brief book examines the sources of Goethe's scientific approach, as can be seen from the titles of the four central chapters: The Neo-Platonic Tradition, The Empirical Tradition, The Rationalistic Tradition, and Goethe's Originality.

Raphael, Alice. *Goethe and the Philosopher's Stone*. London: Routledge and Kegan Paul, 1965.

An examination of key themes in *Faust*, this work is thoroughly influenced by a Jungian perspective.

Salm, Peter. *The Poem as Plant: A Biological View of Goethe's Faust*. Cleveland: The Press of Case Western Reserve University, 1971.

For those desiring a treat in metaphysical thought and cross-disciplinary reflection, this book is a rare pleasure. Religion and science figure in important ways in Salm's vision.

Steiner, Rudolf. *Goethe the Scientist.* Trans. by William Lindeman. Anthroposophic Press, 1986.

Steiner's anthroposophy is an attempt to expand and institutionalize a Goethean world view.

Wilkinson, Elizabeth M., ed. *Goethe Revisited: A Collection of Essays*. New York: Riverrun Press, 1984.

The essays in this anthology look at Goethe's thought from a number of interesting perspectives.

Ten

Kant on Nature and God

Walter Gulick

Kant's impact on discussions of science and religion has been nearly as significant as his revolutionary impact on epistemology, metaphysics, and ethics. His writings set the agenda for much of the philosophical reflection of the nineteenth century. His critique of the three classical arguments for the existence of God continues to provide the standard account with which all subsequent attempts to provide an argument must deal.

Because Kant's writings have formed a sort of watershed in Western philosophy, it is important to be aware of the way his thought developed. There is rich insight in the pre-critical writings as well as in the far better known critical writings. Thus I list the writings of Kant roughly in chronological order (the lectures sometimes span a number of years or cannot be precisely dated).

Kant—Pre-Critical Writings

Universal Natural History and Theory of the Heavens. Trans. with an Intro. by Stanley L. Jaki. Edinburgh: Scottish Academic Press, 1981 [1755].

This cosmogony, setting forth a nebular hypothesis for the creation of the solar system, is thoroughly influenced by the

Newtonian method, yet Kant tries to make physical existence intelligible through a teleological principle, thus reconciling Leibniz with Newton.

"A New Exposition of the First Principles of Metaphysical Knowledge" (*Nova Dilucidatio*). In F. E. England, *Kant's Conception of God*. New York: Humanities Press, 1968 [1755]. Appendix, pp. 213-252.

A discussion of the foundations of metaphysical knowledge in which Kant gropes toward the understanding that the real is not the rational. He discusses the Cartesian version of the ontological proof critically.

The One Possible Basis for a Demonstration of the Existence of God. Trans. with an Intro. by Gordon Treash. New York: Abaris Books, 1979 [1763].

Kant tries to repair the deficiencies in previous versions of the ontological argument by analyzing the conditions for any possibility whatsoever (and not relying on God's perfection).

"Enquiry Concerning the Clarity of the Principles of Natural Theology and Ethics." In *Kant: Selected Pre-Critical Writings and Correspondence with Beck*. Trans. with an Intro. by G. B. Kerferd and D. E. Walford. New York: Barnes & Noble, 1968 [1764].

Kant focusses on problems of method and asserts the intuitional character of geometry.

"On the Form and Principles of the Sensible and Intelligible World" (Inaugural Dissertation). In *Kant: Selected Pre-Critical Writings* (see previous citation), [1770].

Metaphysics seems to be going nowhere, so Kant searches for a new method and distinguishes the sensible world (phenomenal realm of space and time) from the intelligible world of God and his pre-established harmony.

Lectures on Ethics. Trans. by Louis Infeld. New York: Harper Torchbook, 1963 [ca. 1780].

This work contains fascinating details on the role of feeling in the moral life, the errors of religion, and the place of prayer, conscience, friendship, etc. in the ethical life.

Kant – Critical Writings

Critique of Pure Reason. Trans. by Norman Kemp Smith. New York: St. Martin's Press, 1933 [1781, 1787].

There are numerous portions of this great work which bear on science and religion in significant ways.

a) Prefaces to the two editions. Kant previews the scope of the Critique and the dilemmas faced by those pursuing its course: "Human reason has this peculiar fate that in one species of its knowledge it is burdened by questions which, as prescribed by the very nature of reason itself, it is not able to ignore, but which, as transcending all its powers, it is also not able to answer." Kant finds it "necessary to deny knowledge, in order to make room for faith." Kant's Copernican revolution is outlined.

b) Introduction. Analytic and synthetic judgments are distinguished, and Kant explains why synthetic a priori judgments are the key to metaphysical certainty.

c) Transcendental Aesthetic. Space and time are shown to be the forms of intuition to which sensible objects must conform. Our minds create Euclidian space.

d) Idea of a Transcendental Logic. Sensibility is receptive, whereas the understanding is spontaneous. The understanding creates knowledge through a transcendental logic.

e) Transcendental Analytic: Analytic of Concepts. Kant sets forth his argument for the categories, which are the concepts we necessarily and universally employ in thinking about empirical objects. Humans thereby create the Newtonian world to which mathematics applies through their constructive activity in thinking about perceived objects. This section contains the subjective (quasi-psychological) and objective forms of Kant's transcendental deduction of the categories.

f) Analytic of Principles. How are the categories applied to sense data? In this section Kant sets forth the rules of application (either via schemata or principles), whereby thought is linked to sense according to judgments, such as: "In all change of appearances substance is permanent; its quantum in nature is neither increased nor diminished," and "All alterations take place in conformity with the law of the connection of cause and effect."

g) Transcendental Dialectic (A 293, B 349 - A 338, B 396). The nature of reason, which seeks closure in thought through the use of Ideas and inferences, is discussed.

h) The Paralogisms of Pure Reason. This section contains a rather verbose discussion of logical confusion involved in thinking about the self as subject, substance, soul, and the like

i) The Antinomy of Pure Reason. Again Kant is wordy in discussing the conflicting interpretations we fall prey to when we try to bring about completeness in our thought about the world with reference to its origin, composition, and cause. Freedom and necessity are each legitimately used in their proper domains of morality and science respectively.

j) The Ideal of Pure Reason. In this section Kant gives his famous criticisms of the ontological, cosmological, and design arguments for the existence of God.

k) The Final Purpose of the Natural Dialectic of Human Reason (A 669, B 697 - A 704, B 732). Our reason is such that we must assume the existence of a wise Author of the world, but this is a presupposition of thought, a regulative Idea, rather than a Being we know.

l) The Canon of Pure Reason. "All the interests of my reason, speculative as well as practical, combine in the three following questions: 1. What can I know? 2. What ought I to do? 3. What may I hope?" The practical realm (concerning that which may happen through reason) has priority in philosophy over the theoretical realm.

m) The Architectonic of Pure Reason. This section, showing the rationalistic core of Kant's system, is for some reason unduly ignored by those seeking to understand Kant (probably because they long since wearied of the rigors of trying to get through the first *Critique*.).

Prolegomena to any Future Metaphysics. Trans. by Lewis White Beck. Indianapolis: Bobbs-Merrill, 1950 [1783].

The *Prolegomena* provides the easiest entry to Kant's critical thought.

"Idea for a Universal History with a Cosmological Intent." In *Perpetual Peace and Other Essays on Politics, History, and Moral Problems*. Trans. with an Intro. by Ted Humphrey. Indianapolis: Hackett, 1983 [1784], pp. 29-40.

Humans abuse their freedom, but it is in accordance with nature's plan that a perfect civil constitution be developed.

Foundations of the Metaphysics of Morals. Trans. by Lewis White Beck. In *Kant: Selections*. Ed. by Lewis White Beck. New York: Macmillan, 1988 [1785], pp. 244-298.

The categorical imperative in its various forms is developed as the highest criterion by which to judge whether an action is moral (and therefore religious) or not.

Metaphysical Foundations of Natural Science. Trans. by James W. Ellington. Indianapolis: Bobbs-Merrill, 1970 [1786].

In this work Kant moves a step closer toward Newtonian physics from his critical thought. He disagrees with Newton in some respects; he believes absolute space should not be endowed with ontological significance, and he sees matter as not inert but having the motive forces of attraction and repulsion.

His last section is entitled "Metaphysical Foundations of Phenomenology;" "phenomenology" (by which he means a doctrine of appearance) is to have an interesting career in the history of philosophy. Kant planned yet another book connecting his thought to physics. "The Transition from the Metaphysical Foundations of Natural Science to Physics" is among the incomplete works included in the untranslated *Opus Postumus*. Ellington contributes a helpful interpretive essay to this book entitled "The Unity of Kant's Thought in His Philosophy of Corporeal Nature."

"What is Orientation in Thinking?" In *Kant's Critique of Practical Reason and Other Writings in Moral Philosophy.* Trans. with an Intro. by Lewis White Beck. Chicago: University of Chicago Press, 1949 [1786], pp. 293-305.

This brief essay explains how theoretical reason can unmask illusions and practical reason is free to speak of God and set its own laws.

Critique of Practical Reason (see previous citation).

Kant sets forth his moral argument for the existence of God in order to make sense of the human experience of the moral law. The Ideas of God, an intelligible world (the Kingdom of God), and immortality are practical postulates required to make sure that worthiness to be happy is consistent with actual happiness.

Critique of Judgment. Trans. with an Intro. by J. H. Bernard. New York: Hafner, 1951 [1790].

A great work that stands in some tension with the first two *Critiques*, the *Critique of Judgment* explores the way reason may be reflective. Kant's attempt to establish the objective validity of judgments of beauty seems forced. But in the process of exploring the nature of reflective thought, Kant is creative in the way he discusses pleasure and pain, taste, humor, symbols, the sublime, teleology, and other topics.

"On the Failure of All Attempted Philosophical Theodices." Trans. by Michel Despland. In Michel Despland, *Kant on History and Religion*. Montreal: McGill-Queens University Press, 1973 [1791], pp. 283-297.

After exploring the book of Job, Kant states that "theodicy is not a task of science but is a matter of faith."

Religion within the Limits of Reason Alone. Trans. by Theodore M. Greene and Hoyt H. Hudson. New York: Harper & Row, 1960 [1793].

The moral law is understood to have a source, namely, God. Christ is presented as having managed to elicit from us not only obedience to but love of the moral law. However, humans have a disposition toward a self centered radical evil which makes one's inclinations rather than the moral law one's highest good. Humans therefore need salvation. It can be seen that Kant's thought about God and religion develops beyond the ideas he expressed in the second *Critique*. "The Kingdom of God on earth: this is the ultimate vocation of man; Christ led us to it, but one did not understand him and the Kingdom of the priests, not that of God, was set among us." John Silber contributes a major essay explaining the different meanings of will in Kant's ethical thought.

On the Old Saw: That May Be Right in Theory but It Won't Work in Practice. Trans. by E. B. Ashton. Philadelphia: University of Pennsylvania Press, 1974 [1793].

Perhaps the best Kantian work to consult in order to gain a brief overview of how his understanding of human nature, his ethical (and thereby religious) thought, and his socio-political thought cohere.

Anthropology from a Pragmatic Point of View. Trans. by Mary J. Gregor. The Hague: Martinus Nijhoff, 1974 [1798].

This work allows one to see the human rather than the super-rational or ethereal Kant. One finds that feelings and emotions do have an important role in life for Kant.

Logic. Trans. with an Intro. by Robert S. Hartman and Wolfgang Schwartz. Indianapolis: Bobbs-Merrill, 1974 [1800].

These lecture notes are wonderfully illuminating for someone wishing to comprehend the logical foundations of Kant's thought. Logic is understood by Kant in a broad sense. The translators' one hundred page introduction is a treasure chest full of insightful explanations as to how Kant thought and what he meant.

Lectures on Philosophical Theology. Trans. by Allen W. Wood and Gertrude M. Clark. Ithaca: Cornell University Press, 1978 [first published in 1817].

These lectures are thought to date from 1783-84, which would explain why they cover much of the same material found in the first *Critique*. They show a thorough familiarity with Hume's *Dialogues Concerning Natural Religion*.

Secondary Sources on Kant

Allison, Henry E. *Kant's Transcendental Idealism: An Interpretation and Defense*. New Haven: Yale University Press, 1983.

A thorough, reliable, up to date analysis of the *Critique of Pure Reason.*

Beck, Lewis White. *A Commentary on Kant's Critique of Practical Reason.* Chicago: University of Chicago Press, 1960.

This commentary reveals how useful an analysis of a single work can be. Beck in his many essays and books can be counted upon to be sympathetic, historically informed, and insightful.

Barth, Karl. *Protestant Thought: From Rousseau to Ritschl.* Trans. by Brian Cozens. New York: Harper & Brothers, 1959.

Chapter Four, pp. 150-196, deals with Kant in a fair but critical manner. "The Kantian enterprise consists in a great 'if...then' sentence: if the reality of religion is confined to that which, as religion within the limits of reason alone, is subjected to the self-critique of reason, then religion is that which is fitting to the ideally practical nature of pure reason, and that only."

Brittan, Gordon G., Jr. *Kant's Theory of Science.* Princeton: Princeton University Press, 1978.

An interpretation written from the point of view of contemporary analytic philosophy.

Buchdahl, Gerd. *Metaphysics and the Philosophy of Science.* Cambridge, MA: The MIT Press, 1969.

This masterful study (some 700 pages of compact analysis) deserves to be far better known than it is. Buchdahl explores science in the thought of Descartes, Locke, Berkeley, Hume, Leibniz and especially Kant. Reason, rather than understanding, is emphasized to be the proper locus of science in Kant.

Cassirer, Ernst. *Kant's Life and Thought*. Trans. by James Haden. New Haven: Yale University Press, 1981 [first published in German in 1918].

Cassirer has written an accessible intellectual biography which places Kant's thought clearly in its historical milieu.

Collins, James D. *The Emergence of Philosophy of Religion*. New Haven: Yale University Press, 1967.

Collins' justified reputation for clear critical analysis could have been established solely by the section of this book dealing with Kant. The richness of Kant's thought about religion is brought alive.

Deleuze, Gilles. *Kant's Critical Philosophy: The Doctrine of the Faculties*. Trans. by Hugh Tomlinson and Barbara Habberjam. Minneapolis: University of Minnesota Press, 1984.

In the 77 pages of this work, Deleuze, a French philosopher of weight in his own right, penetrates into the structure of Kant's thought by explaining Kant's pregnant notion of the faculties, which is all too often facilely dismissed as an embarrassing example of psychologism. Deleuze concludes that for Kant (anticipating Hegel) it is "the concept of freedom which is realized or accomplished in nature. The accomplishment of freedom and of the good Sovereign in the sensible world thus implies an original synthetic activity of man: *History* is this accomplishment."

Despland, Michel. *Kant on History and Religion*. Montreal: McGill-Queen's University Press, 1973.

If one is seeking a clear exposition of Kant's systematic thought about the religious life, this is an excellent source.

Findlay, J. N. *Kant and the Transcendental Object*. Oxford: Clarendon Press, 1981.

Findlay offers a comprehensive account of Kant's transcendental idealism from its pre-critical origins to the writing Kant left unfinished at his death.

Heidegger, Martin. *Kant and the Problem of Metaphysics*. Trans. by James S. Churchill. Bloomington: Indiana University Press, 1962.

This is one of those happy works such that when one reads it one gains significant insight into both the person being described and the author writing the exposition. In 1950 Heidegger, over twenty years after he wrote the book, too easily acknowledged what some critics had claimed: that he had gone astray with the violence of his interpretation. In fact, this is a brilliant, creative reading of the metaphysical grounding of Kant's thought.

Heimsoeth, Heinz. "Metaphysical Motives in the Development of Critical Idealism." In Moltke S. Gram, *Kant: Disputed Questions*. Trans. and ed. by Moltke S. Gram. Chicago: Quadrangle Books, 1967.

Heimsoeth is one of this century's foremost German Kant scholars, and this article is typical of his historically sensitive treatments of Kant.

Jaspers, Karl. *Kant*. Taken from *Great Philosophers*, Vol. I, part 3. Trans by Ralph Manheim. San Diego: Harcourt Brace Jovanovich, 1966.

Jaspers explores Kant from a holistic perspective which is a helpful corrective to the partial "Kant's Theory of. . . " studies which abound.

Kroner, Richard. *Kant's Weltanschauung*. Trans. by John E. Smith. Chicago: University of Chicago Press, 1956 (German original published in 1914).

This brief work on Kant's ethical world view is still helpful. "Kant holds that the recognition of an imperative, guiding us not only when we seek the truth but guiding our will as its highest measure and goal, brings us nearer to the ultimate meaning of the world than any speculative or theoretical knowledge possibly could."

Martin, Gottfried. *Kant's Metaphysics and Theory of Science*. Trans. by P. G. Lucas. Manchester: Manchester University Press, 1955.

There are sections on "Nature" and "The being of God" in this work, which relates Kant's thought to the philosophical and scientific context of his time.

McFarlane, J. D. *Kant's Concept of Teleology*. Edinburgh: University of Edinburgh Press, 1970.

McFarlane focuses his discussion primarily on the second half of the *Critique of Judgment*.

Paton, H. J. *The Categorical Imperative: A Study in Kant's Moral Philosophy*. Chicago: University of Chicago Press, 1948.

"In his application of moral principles Kant takes into account most fully the desires and purposes and potentialities of men, and indeed . . . it is on a teleological view of man and of the universe that application of moral principles is based." Paton, one of the grand old men of recent Kant scholarship, shows that Kant does take account of consequences in his ethical thought.

Pitte, Frederick P. van de. *Kant as Philosophical Anthropologist.* The Hague: Martinus Nijhoff, 1971.

This book makes a good case for the usefulness of looking at Kant as a philosophical anthropologist.

Raschke, Carl A. *Moral Action, God, and History in the Thought of Immanuel Kant.* Missoula, MT: Scholars Press, 1975.

Raschke looks at such issues as Kant's notion of intentionality, God as a moral agent, and autonomy and theonomy.

Rescher, Nicholas. *The Primacy of Practice.* Oxford: Basil Blackwell, 1973.

Rescher brings logical sophistication to his analysis of practical reason.

Strawson, P. F. *The Bounds of Sense: An Essay on Kant's 'Critique of Pure Reason.'* London: Methuen, 1966.

One of the leading English analysts examines the first third of the first *Critique* in a generally sympathetic treatment of Kant as an epistemologist.

Vleeschauwer, Herman-J. de. *The Development of Kantian Thought.* Trans. by A. R. C. Duncan. London: Thomas Nelson and Sons, 1962.

This is still one of the indispensable studies of how Kant's thought developed in both his pre-critical and critical stages of thought.

Werkmeister, W. H. *Kant: The Architectonic and Development of His Philosophy*. LaSalle, IL: Open Court Publishing Company, 1980.

While Werkmeister's writing style can be rather ponderous, the use of Kant's architectonic as a clue to comprehending his thought is helpful.

Wood, Allen W. *Kant's Rational Theology*. Ithaca, NY: Cornell University Press, 1978.

"We cannot, I realized, have a full or balanced understanding of Kant's thought on religious subjects so long as we fail to take account of his reflections, often exceedingly abstract, obscure, and subtle, concerning the rational origin, content, and status of our concept of a supreme being." This book complements Wood's earlier book on the moral aspects of Kant's religious philosophy, *Kant's Moral Religion*.

Eleven

Concepts of Nature and God: Kierkegaard to Dostoevsky

William J. Garland

Soren Kierkegaard (1813-1855)

A. Primary Sources.

A Kierkegaard Anthology. Ed. Robert Bretall. Princeton University Press, 1947.

An excellent collection of excerpts from Kierkegaard's major works, including *Either/Or, Concluding Unscientific Postscript,* and *Training in Christianity.*

Kierkegaard's Writings. Ed. Howard V. Hong. 25 volumes. Princeton: Princeton University Press, 1978.

This series consists in new translations of Kierkegaard's works from the best Danish edition of the text. It is an indispensable aid to Kierkegaard scholarship.

Either/Or: A Fragment of Life. 2 vols. Trans. David F. Swenson and Lillian Marvin Swenson. Princeton: Princeton University Press and London: Humphrey Milford, Oxford University Press, 1944.

A long and rambling portrait of the difference between the aesthetic stage of life and the ethical stage. The title expresses Kierkegaard's conviction that life continually presents us with forced options rather than materials for synthesis.

Fear and Trembling, in *Fear and Trembling and The Sickness Unto Death.* Trans. Walter Lowrie. Garden City, New York: Doubleday, 1954.

A dramatic presentation of the difference between the ethical stage of life and the religious stage. Kiekegaard relates the story of God's command to Abraham to kill his son Issac to his own view of the radical nature of religious faith.

Philosophical Fragments. Trans. Howard V. Hong and Edna H. Hong. Princeton: Princeton University Press, 1985.

This work sets the stage for the *Concluding Unscientific Postscript* by stating but not answering Kierkegaard's basic question about Truth: is truth something which has always existed in a latent form within us (as Socrates thought) or something that we must receive from a Teacher who posses the truth that we do not have? The latter view is the view of Christianity, but Kierkegaard does not fully embrace this view.

Stages on Life's Way. Trans. Walter Lowrie. Introduction by Paul Sponheim. New York: Schucken Books, 1967.

A full exposition of the three stages or "spheres of existence" – the aesthetic, the ethical and the religious. The exposition of the religious stage in Quidam's Diary is long and tedious and would probably be rather boring to most readers. The most famous part of the book is "The Banquet," which depicts the pursuit of pleasure in the aesthetic stage of existence.

Concluding Unscientific Postscript. Trans. David F. Swenson. Princeton: Princeton University Press, 1941.

This work is perhaps Kierkegaard's fullest exposition of the radical implications of his philosophical standpoint. He gives a sharp critique of objective thinking and defends the irreducibly subjective dimension of truth. Kierkegaard is especially concerned with religious truth and the "Absolute Paradox" of Christianity—the fact that the eternal God has come to be in time.

The Present Age and *Of the Difference Between a Genius and an Apostle.* Trans. Alexander Dru. New York: Harper and Row, 1962.

The Present Age is a criticism of the tendency towards social conformity and the neglect of the plight of the solitary individual. *Of the Difference Between a Genius and an Apostle* contrasts the way of life of the few individuals who are endowed with special talents (the geniuses) with the way of life which is open to anyone—that of becoming an apostle of Christ.

Works of Love. Trans. David F. Swenson and Lillian Marvin Swenson. Port Washington: Kennikat Press, 1972.

Here Kierkegaard attempts to explain what is meant by the Christian duty to love our neighbors as we love ourselves. He connects Christian love with our actions towards others rather than with our feelings towards them, but he places this Kantian conception of love within the intensely personal context of our relationship to God.

The Sickness Unto Death. Trans. Howard V. Hong and Edna H. Hong. Princeton: Princeton University Press, 1980.

This is a penetrating psychological analysis of the concept of despair, which Kierkegaard calls the "sickness unto death." Kierkegaard claims that Christian faith is the only cure for despair and he enthusiastically endorses the Christian way of life.

Training In Christianity. Trans. Walter Lowrie. Princeton: Princeton University Press, 1947.

This work concentrates upon Kierkegaard's central question – what does it mean to be a Christian? His answer is that being a Christian involves the adoption of a new way of life. To be a Christian is to become contemporaneous with Christ in his suffering and humiliation even though they offend us morally and intellectually. Kierkegaard relates these claims to his fundamental epistemological view that truth is subjectivity.

B. Secondary Sources.

Collins, James. *The Mind of Kierkegaard.* Chicago: Henry Regnery Company, 1953.

This is a comprehensive and insightful commentary on the central themes in Kierkegaard's philosophy. Collins relates the views of Kierkegaard to the views of other thinkers in the history of western philosophy.

Swenson, David F. *Something About Kierkegaard.* Ed. Lillian Marvin Swenson. Minneapolis: Augsburg Publishing House, 1945.

This is a collection of essays by the pioneer of Kierkegaard scholarship in America. Swenson's papers are especially valuable for their explanation of Kierkegaard's existential dialectic and for their analysis of the three stages of human existence.

Lowrie, Walter. *Kierkegaard.* New York: Oxford University Press, 1938.

This is a thorough and detailed study of the life and thought of Kierkegaard. It presents a portrait of Kierkegaard's psychological and spiritual development which provides valuable insight into his written works.

Elrod, John W. *Being and Existence in Kierkegaard's Pseudonymous Works.* Princeton: Princeton University Press, 1975.

The author argues that Kierkegaard's pseudonymous works contain an ontology which serves as a unifying principle for understanding his claim that there are three stages of human existence—the aesthetic, the ethical and the religious.

Dunning, Stephen N. *Kierkegaard's Dialectic of Inwardness.* Princeton: Princeton University Press, 1985.

The author claims that there are dialectical structures which permeate Kierkegaard's view of the self in his pseudonymous works and which enable us to give a coherent account of his theory of the three stages of life. At issue here is the presence of an unconscious element of Hegelianism in Kierkegaard's thought.

Friedrich Nietzsche (1844-1900)

A. Primary Sources.

The Portable Nietzsche. Trans. Walter Kaufmann. New York: Viking Press, 1954.

Contains complete versions of *Thus Spake Zarathustra, Twilight of the Idols, The Antichrist,* and *Nietzsche contra Wagner.* Short selections from other works.

The Basic Writings of Nietzsche. Ed. Walter Kaufmann. New York: Random House, 1968.

Contains complete versions of *The Birth of Tragedy, Beyond Good and Evil, On the Genealogy of Morals, The Case of Wagner,* and *Ecce Homo* with some commentary.

The Philosophy of Nietzsche. Ed. Geoffrey Clive. New York: New American Library, 1965.

A strategic selection of passages from most of Nietzsche's main writings. One practical problem is that the print is small and difficult to read.

The Birth of Tragedy, in *The Birth of Tragedy* and *The Genealogy of Morals.* Trans. Francis Golffing. Garden City, New York: Doubleday, 1956.

Here Nietzsche claims that the genius of Greek tragedy lies in the synthesis of the Apollonian and the Dionysian elements in human life. This view contrasts with the previous views of the Greeks as serene, calm and completely rational; Nietzsche calls attention to the Dionysian passion which lies beneath the Apollonian orderliness of Greek tragedy.

"On Truth and Lies in a Nonmoral Sense," in *Philosophy and Truth: Selections from Nietzsche's Notebooks of the Early 1870's.* Trans. David Breazeale. Atlantic Highlands, New Jersey: Humanities Press, 1979.

This seminal essay on the nature of knowledge was found among Nietzsche's unpublished manuscripts and was probably written in 1873. Here Nietzsche presents a devastating critique of the traditional theory of objective knowledge and concludes that "truths are illusions which we have forgotten are illusions." On Nietzsche's view, our "truths" are just as illusory as our "lies," but the "truths" are those fictions which are more *useful* in preserving and enhancing human life.

Human, All Too Human. Trans. R. J. Hollingdale. Cambridge: Cambridge University Press, 1986.

This book marks Nietzsche's decision to turn away from essays to aphorisms as the vehicle for expressing his claim that there are no facts but only interpretations. Thus begins his psychological analysis of the "truths" of both science and religion as value perspectives which differ only in "rank," not in objective reference.

Daybreak. Trans. R. J. Hollingdale. Cambridge: Cambridge University Press, 1982.

A book of aphorisms on a variety of subjects, such as religion, friendship, the nature of philosophy, the origin of morality, and the torments of the soul. Sections 76 (on evil) and 542 (on philosophy) are noteworthy.

The Gay Science (sometimes called *Joyful Wisdom*). Trans. Walter Kaufmann. New York: Random House, 1974.

Another book of aphorisms in which Nietzsche applauds the way in which the quest for knowledge builds human character but continues to insist that all knowledge is essentially perspectival. His remarks about man's quest for certainty in Sections 2 and 347 are noteworthy; also, Section 125 on "The Madman" announces the death of God.

Thus Spake Zarathustra. Trans. R. J. Hollingdale. Baltimore: Penguin Books, 1969.

This is probably Nietzsche's masterpiece. He presents in narrative form the main themes of his mature philosophy: the death of God, the subordination of truth to the will, the universality of the will to power, the necessity for the creation of new values, the Overman, and the celebration of the joy of existence. Nietzsche's mouthpiece here is the ancient prophet Zoroaster (Zarathustra).

Beyond Good and Evil. Trans. Walter Kaufmann. New York: Vintage Books, 1966.

This is still essentially a book of aphorisms, but the aphorisms are longer and more developed. Nietzsche comments on the nature of knowledge, religion, morality, and art, and he gives his picture of the Overman in Part 9.

On the Genealogy of Morals, in *On the Genealogy of Morals* and *Ecce Homo.* Trans. Walter Kaufmann and R. J. Hollingdale. New York: Vintage Books, 1967.

This book consists of three essays on the "origins" of morality, in which Nietzsche contrasts the aristocratic morality of the Greeks with the slave morality of Christianity. The first two essays give his analysis of the natural history of morality.

Twilight of the Idols in *Twilight of the Idols* and *The Anti-Christ.* Trans. R. J. Hollingdale. Harmondsworth, Middlesex, England: Penguin Books, 1968.

Here Nietzsche sums up many of his concerns during the past ten years—his attitude towards Socrates, the ways in which philosophers deceive themselves, the four great errors in thinking (compare Bacon's Idols), the nature of art and morality, and the evils of the modern age.

The Anti-Christ, in *Twilight of the Idols* and *The Anti-Christ.* Trans. R. J. Hollingdale. Harmondsworth, Middlesex, England: Penguin Books, 1968.

This book gathers together Nietzsche's thoughts about the Christian religion and Christian morality and presents a scathing attack on all Christian beliefs and values. It ends with a call for the revaluation of all values.

The Will to Power. Trans. Walter Kaufmann and R. J. Hollingdale. Ed. Walter Kaufmann. New York: Random House, 1967.

This is a collection of manuscripts organized and edited after Nietzsche's death around the general theme of "The Will to Power." Part I contains Nietzsche's reflections on nihilism; Part II contains his critique of moral, religious and philosophical values. Part III compares the method of science with the method of art, while Part IV presents Nietzsche's vision of the Overman, Dionysus and the eternal recurrence.

B. Secondary Sources.

Kaufmann, Walter. *Nietzsche: Philosopher, Psychologist, Antichrist.* Princeton: Princeton University Press, 1950.

This is a thorough, detailed, and well-documented study of the development of Nietzsche's thought and its culmination in a philosophy of the will to power. Kaufmann tries to tone down some of Nietzsche's more radical assertions about exerting power over other people.

Morgan, George A. *What Nietzsche Means.* Cambridge: Harvard University Press, 1941.

This is a comprehensive and well-balanced treatment of the more systematic aspects of Nietzsche's thought. Morgan sees the metaphysical elements in Nietzsche's philosophy but misses the thrust of his radical critique of metaphysics.

Danto, Arthur C. *Nietzsche as Philosopher.* New York: Macmillan Publishing Co., 1967.

Danto gives a critique of Nietzsche's thought from the standpoint of analytic philosophy. He finds many contradictions in Nietzsche but claims that a coherent system of thought can be uncovered in *Beyond Good and Evil.*

Heidegger, Martin. *Nietzsche.* Vol. 1 and Vol. 2. Trans. David F. Krell. New York: Harper and Row, 1979-84.

________________. *Nietzsche.* Vol. 3. Ed. David F. Krell. Trans. Joan Stombaugh and Frank A. Capuzzi. New York: Harper and Row, forthcoming.

________________. *Nietzsche.* Vol. 4. Trans. Frank Capuzzi. New York: Harper and Row, 1982.

These are the current translations available in English of Martin Heidegger's monumental and controversial interpretation of many aspects of Nietzsche's thought.

Lampert, Laurence. *Nietzsche's Teaching.* New Haven and London: Yale University Press, 1986.

This is a comprehensive interpretation of *Thus Spake Zarathustra* as the key to what Nietzsche rejects in previous moral, philosophical and religious views and to what he puts forth as an affirmative alternative for human life.

Yovel, Yirmiyahu, ed. *Nietzsche as Affirmative Thinker.* Dordrecht: Martinus Nijhoff, 1986.

A collection of essays from a 1983 conference on Nietzsche in Jerusalem. Of particular interest are the essays dealing with Nietzsche's "method of genealogy" and contemporary hermeneutics.

Fyodor Dostoevsky (1821-1881)

A. Primary Works.

Notes From Underground. Trans. Constance Garnett. New York: Hermitage Press, 1967.

Here Dostoevsky first touches on the great themes that he will explore in the major novels that follow – freedom of the will, the rational organization of human happiness (as symbolized by the Crystal Palace), and the value of suffering. He also sets up the dilemma of modern man: either happiness at the expense of free will or free will at the expense of happiness.

Crime and Punishment. Trans. Constance Garnett. New York: Random House, 1956.

This novel deals with the question of free will within the context of the concept of crime. Dostoevsky's thesis is that a free act is a criminal act in the sense of an act which goes beyond what is permitted by law and by custom. He also connects the act of committing a crime with the desire of the criminal to be caught and punished for it. This complex motivation characterizes the "hero" Raskolnikov, who murders a pawnbroker but finds redemption at the end through the love of a prostitute.

The Idiot. Trans. Constance Garnett. New York: Macmillan, 1948.

This is a complex and rambling story centered around the figure of Prince Myshkin, who is in one sense a Christ figure in his gentleness and compassion but in another sense a dim-wit who is lacking in practical common-sense. The Prince fails to redeem the other characters with whom he interacts, but he does offer the other characters a glimpse of their own possibilities for goodness.

The Possessed. Trans. Constance Garnett. New York: Random House, 1948.

This complex psychological and sociological drama centers around the character of Nikolay Stavrogin, who exemplifies the devastating consequences of choosing human freedom while denying God. Stavrogin recognizes no objective value distinctions; he only recognizes the brute force of human wills. The collision of these wills leads to the destruction of those around him and finally to his own suicide. The novel contains a few hints of how redemption is possible.

The Brothers Karamazov. Trans. Constance Garnett. New York: Random House, 1950.

This is Dostoevsky's masterpiece in both his statement of basic philosophical dilemmas and in the unfolding of a powerful and complex psychological drama. The dramatic theme of the right of a son to rebel against his father parallels the philosophical theme of the right of human beings to rebel against God. The philosophical heart of the novel is the chapter "Pro and Contra," which contains Ivan's rebellion against unjust suffering and the legend of the Grand Inquisitor. Here the demands of reason and happiness collide directly with the demands of religious faith and freedom.

Notes From Underground and *The Grand Inquisitor.* Selection, trans. and introduction by Ralph E. Matlaw. New York: Dutton, 1960.

A useful combination of *Notes From Underground* with the most philosophically significant portion of *The Brothers Karamazov.*

B. Secondary Sources.

Wasiolek, Edward. *Dostoevsky: The Major Fiction.* Cambridge: The MIT Press, 1964.

Perhaps the best guide to the paradoxical nature of the characters which appear in Dostoevsky's "great novels." Wasiolek seeks to show how the author's ideas are integrally connected with the artistic structure of his works.

Berdyaev, Nicholas. *Dostoievsky.* London: Sheed and Ward, 1934.

This is an interpretation of the religious thought of Dostoevsky from the standpoint of a leading Christian Existentialist who came to Europe from Russia during the 1920's. It is not a scholarly analysis of texts but an attempt to convey the spirit of Dostoevsky's religious vision. There is an interesting chapter (Chapter VIII) on the legend of the Grand Inquisitor.

Lord, Robert. *Dostoevsky: Essays and Perspectives.* Berkeley and Los Angeles: University of California Press, 1970.

This is a collection of essays by a British scholar on specific aspects of Dostoevsky's life and thought. The essay called "The Temptation of Philosophy" treats the interconnected themes of paradox and freedom in Kierkegaard and Dostoevsky.

Jones, Malcolm V. *Dostoyevsky: The Novel of Discord.* London: Elek Books, 1976.

An imaginative interpretation of Dostoevsky's major novels in terms of the fundamental tension between chaos and the search for a principle of order. Jones claims that there is an interrelationship between philosophical ideas and the development of dramatic themes.

Jackson, Robert L. ed. *Dostoevsky: New Perspectives.* Englewood Cliffs, New Jersey: Prentice-Hall, 1984.

A collection of important essays in Dostoevsky by recent critics from Eastern Europe, Western Europe and the United States. Especially noteworthy are the essays by Robert Louis Jackson, "Aristotelian Movement and Design in Part Two of *Notes From Underground,*" and Jacques Catteau, "The Paradox of the Legend of the Grand Inquisitor."

Twelve

Resources for Teaching Hegel's Philosophy

Stanley Riukas

A. Primary sources

Hegel, G. W. F., *The Philosophy of Hegel*, ed. Carl J. Friedrich, Modern Library, 1965.

This anthology I have found very useful in my 19th Century Philosophy course, in which I devote about one third of time to the discussion of Hegel's philosophy. The book contains substantial and judiciously chosen selections (up to 100 pages and more) from Hegel's major works such as *Phenomenology of Mind*, *Philosophy of History*, *Philosophy of Right*, *Philosophy of Art, and the Logic* in addition to shorter selections from *History of Philosophy*, *Philosophy of Nature*, and others. With the general introduction to Hegel's philosophy and with special introductions to each of its major parts as well as with regular classroom analyses of the crucial texts, students, as a rule, find most of the selections manageable and even admirable for their thoroughness and profundity. In 15 class hours a great deal can be accomplished with the help of anthology like this. But when I tried once to us it in History of Modern Philosophy course, where only 6 class hours were available for Hegel's philosophy, the results were somewhat less impressive since much of the book had to remain untouched. Its wealth was simply overwhelming.

________, *Lectures on the Philosophy of History*, trans. by J. Sibree, Dover, 1956.

With the possible exception of the writings of the young Hegel, Hegel's *Philosophy of History* is perhaps the single most readable book. It presupposes only a limited amount of Hegel's general metaphysics, present in his *Logic* or in his *Philosophy of Spirit* and perhaps more present in his *Philosophy of Nature*, and it has a perfectly transparent structure. I have used it occasionally in my 19th Century Philosophy course (15 hours) with satisfactory but not impressive results for the simple reason that it did not seem to provide enough variety for a 5-week haul. On the other hand, I have used it with great success in my History of Modern Philosophy courses, where the amount of time is only 5 or 6 hours and where the book gives plenty to do with the students without losing its novelty. But obviously 6 hours or even 15 hours is such a small amount of time that it does not even begin to exhaust the wealth of ideas and insights contained in this book.

__________, *The Phenomenology of Mind*, trans. by J. B. Baillie, New York: Macmillan, 1910.

This masterpiece of Hegel's philosophy has notoriously been dubbed as the most difficult work of the entire philosophical literature. The prosaic truth however, is that it is probably no more difficult than any major work by a major thinker. The only thing that can be truthfully said about it is that it is more complex because it deals with a larger number of interrelated themes than most similar works. The *Phenomenology* was intended to accomplish a double task: to give a first, fresh and inspired, statement of Hegel's entire philosophy as well as to provide a truly comprehensive (700 pages!) introduction to his entire philosophical system yet to be formulated and elaborated. Accordingly, there is a pretty close parallel between the structure of *Phenomenology* and that of the System or *Encyclopedia of Philosophical Sciences*, as some commentators have noted. Thus Hegel touches on practically all major themes of his philosophy such as Logic, Metaphysics, Epistemology, Philosophy of Nature, Philosophy of Mind, Political and Moral Philosophy, Philosophy of Art, Philosophy of Religion, and Philosophy of Philosophy. All these "themes" or disciplines are subordinate to the central theme of the *Phenomenology*, which is the development of Mind or Spirit in its three-fold dimension: the subjective mind, the objective mind, and the absolute mind. I have used the *Phenomenology* more than once in my Senior Seminar in philosophy with considerable success. My method was to begin the Seminar with a comprehensive general introduction to Hegel's philosophy, 3 or 4 class hours in length, as well as the introduction to the *Phenomenology*. The study of *Phenomenology* itself consisted of brief introductions to carefully chosen crucial texts along with reading assignments. After students had read these texts at home, I analyzed the more difficult or more important parts of them in the classroom until students had a pretty good idea of their meaning taken by themselves and in the context of Hegel's philosophy. It is a difficult job, but it has also some rewards, and I may be using this book again when I am asked to conduct that Seminar.

______, *Lectures on the Philosophy of Religion,* trans. by P. C Brown et al., Berkeley: University of California Press, 1984.

This is a fascinating book on the nature of religion, including what Hegel calls "the revealed religion," meaning Christianity. As is known, this book contains a detailed and systematic elaboration of one of the parts of *The Philosophy of Spirit*, which is the third great division of Hegel's philosophical system presented in his *Encyclopedia*, in the part or chapter on Religion. Hegel shows here how the religious dimension of the human mind evolves through 3 basic stages (and a number of sub-stages) from Natural religion through religion of Art to the Revealed religion. These three stages correspond to the three stages of the unfolding human spirit in the course of history. This book is too voluminous for a 6-week or even 15-week "module course" on Hegel's philosophy, and too restricted in content for a whole semester course. however, I have often used its excellent (concise and lucid) Introduction of 100 plus pages in my History of Modern Philosophy course (6 hours to Hegel) in combination with the Introductions to both Philosophy of Art and to History of Philosophy, which latter Introduction gives Hegel's view of the nature of philosophy. These three Introductions were available until recently in a paperback, *Hegel on Art, Religion, and Philosophy*, by Harper Torchbooks. Combined with a selection on Hegel's *Philosophy of History* contained in the Mentor paperback, *The Age of Ideology*, these three Introductions convey a pretty good idea of some major points of Hegel's philosophy.

______, *The Phenomenology of Spirit*, trans. by A. v. Miller, Oxford: Clarendon Press, 1977.

This is the same book as the *Phenomenology of Mind*, translated by J. B. Baillie in 1910 and discussed above, except that it is more recently translated and, in some passages, is more accurate while obviously it fails to attain the perfection of the original. Its greatest advantage is that it reads like a book written in contemporary English.

______, *The Philosophy of Fine Art*, trans. by F.P.B. Osmaston, London, G. Bell & Sons, 1920.

This work constitutes Hegel's elaboration, detailed and systematic, of the *Philosophy of Spirit*'s section "On Art." Like Religion, Art passes through three stages (and a number of sub-stages), the Oriental stage, the Classical Stage, and the Romantic stage, which, again like in Religion, correspond to the three stages of the general history of man. Again like *Philosophy of Religion, Philosophy of Fine Art* is too voluminous for use in undergraduate courses, where only a few hours normally can be devoted to Hegel and it is too limited in content for use in a full-semester undergraduate course. Fortunately again, this book like most of his works contains one of those famous Hegelian "Introductions" where in 100 pages or so Hegel gives a concise and lucid exposition of the very essence of fine art. This is a text that is quite easily accessible to undergraduates (I mean philosophy majors), and I have had no problems when using it in History of Modern Philosophy courses. It was until recently available, as noted above, in the Harper Torchbook, *Hegel on Art, Religion, and Philosophy*, in combination with Introductions to *Religion* and to *History of Philosophy*. This Introduction to *Art* is also contained in *Philosophy of Hegel*, ed. Carl J. Friedrich and *Hegel Selections*, available from Scribner.

______, *Philosophy of Right*, trans. by T. M. Knox, Oxford, Clarendon Press, 1949.

This is the fourth and last of Hegel's major works published during his lifetime and it contains his exposition of his political philosophy and of certain aspects of his ethical theory, if one can speak at all of his ethical or moral theory. With just about 200 pages in length, this in undoubtedly the shortest major work published by Hegel. In a way, this is the most pedestrian of Hegel's works. Its very brevity suggests that Hegel does not have much to say about the State. He explicitly rejects the idea that the political philosophy should tell us what the State, the Ideal State, ought to be. His political philosophy, he contends, is therefore not to be viewed as a reformist *Programschrift* or a utopia, but only as a description of a fairly decent contemporary state with which he is intimately familiar. Disarmingly, he declares that Philosophy always comes too late onto the political scene to do anything more than to describe, to analyze, and thus to understand what is already there – to understand is the destiny of Philosophy in the domain of politics and in every other sphere of the spirit rather than to "change things," as Marx was to postulate. This book is quite accessible to philosophy majors if 15 hours of time are available, though I myself have never used it. But I might use it.

Fichte, J. G., *The Vocation of Man*, trans. by W. Smith, LaSalle: Open Court Publishers. 1965. This is perhaps the most charming of Fichte's works. In just about 150 pages he gives a concise, popular, and eloquent exposition of his Idealistic Philosophy, stating his views about God, the world, and man's destiny in the world. Like Socrates, he brings down philosophy from heavens and expresses it in terms of everyday moral concerns, thus showing that Philosophy, in addition to its theoretical side, has also – and of necessity – a practical side. I have used this book a few times in my 19th Century Philosophy course, where at least 2 or 3 class hours are available for Fichte's philosophy. I would not dream of using it in my introductory courses – except maybe a few pages, if easily available in some Introductory text.

________, *Science of Knowledge*, trans. by P. Heath and J. Lachs, New York: Cambridge University Press, 1982.

This book is Fichte's technical exposition of his entire philosophical system and has gone through a number of editions during his lifetime. The 1804 version has attained a semi-official standing and is the one here translated by Heath & Lachs. This is no easy book, but it could be used as one of principal texts in an undergraduate course on German Idealist Philosophy along with Schelling's *The Ages of the World*, and Hegel's *Phenomenology*, or *Philosophy of Spirit*.

Schelling F. W. J., *The Ages of the World*, trans. by F. deW. Bolman, Jr., New York: AMS Press, 1967 (1942).

This work is undoubtedly one of the greatest philosophical masterpieces of all times. In hardly more than 150 pages, Schelling gives a comprehensive and profound exposition of his philosophical system at the nearly final stage of its development, and he does this in the style that is at the same time prophetic, poetic, and philosophic. Although thoughts discussed there are most fundamental, God, the world, man, and the manifold relations among them, the book reads almost as if it were the book of Genesis or some other familiar biblical text. God and the world are seen to be mutually inseparable and to be caught in the process of development through stages. This book, too, could profitably be used in a course on German Idealist Philosophy along with Fichte's *Science of Knowledge* and Hegel's *Phenomenology* or *Philosophy of Spirit*, as noted above.

B. Secondary sources

Findlay, J .N., *The Philosophy of Hegel : An Introduction and Re-Examination*, New York: Collier Books, 1964

While this book is principally intended to serve as a thoughtful and rather easily readable introduction to Hegel's philosophy, mainly for undergraduate students, it is sufficiently challenging even to graduate students and the instructors themselves, especially where it deals with "re-examination" of certain popular interpretations of Hegel's philosophy such as the view that Hegel is an idealist rather than materialist. Findlay presents rather impressive arguments in favor of a materialistic interpretation of Hegel's philosophy without appealing to Feuerbach's arguments as Marx did. It is a useful and thought-provoking book to be referred to from time to time during the semester.

Kaufmann, W. A., *Hegel: Reinterpretation, Texts, and Commentary*, Garden City, N.Y.: Doubleday, 1965.

The chief merit of this book is that it provides a number of excellent samples of a truly scholarly interpretation (or "reinterpretation") of Hegel's philosophy solidly based on a careful analysis of a few crucial texts. With a superlative mastery of both German and English, Kaufmann has little difficulty in showing how most English writers on Hegel have gone astray in the interpretation (read, "misinterpretation") of Hegel because of their inadequate mastery of German of the early nineteenth century. The book sets an example of a truly scholarly exegesis of Hegelian texts and of an interpretation ("reinterpretation") based on it. It is useful for both undergraduates and graduates.

Stace, W.T., *The Philosophy of Hegel: A Systematic Exposition*, New York: Dover, 1955.

The chief merit of this work is suggested by its very title: "a systematic exposition." It is a superb exposition of the Hegelian philosophic system based on the essentially traditional interpretation of it as a form of idealism. Delightfully lucid and concise, even in its external organization it follows and reflects the structure of the Hegelian system as it is articulated in the *Encyclopedia*, and elaborated in other works dealing with specific philosophic disciplines as parts of the *Philosophy of Spirit*. It is to be viewed as a fairly standard text among those which attempt to introduce a beginner to Hegel's philosophy. It should precede consultation of both Findlay's and Kaufmann's books.

Fackenheim, Emil L., *The Religious Dimension of Hegel's Thought*, Chicago: Chicago Univ. Press, 1967.

The author writes lucidly and concisely and has no difficulty in showing that religion permeates Hegel's thought from beginning to the end and thus makes him the most "God-intoxicated" man. However, in spite of the pervasiveness of religion, Fackenheim does not view Hegel's philosophy as a form of pantheism. Rather he views Hegel's God as fully transcendent to the world in the same sense in which Jewish and Christian religions regard God as transcendent. While undoubtedly many of Hegel's texts can be adduced to support this interpretation, many more of his texts equally, if not more strongly, suggest a pantheistic or, more likely, an atheistic interpretation. It is a helpful book to those who wish to attain to a deeper view of Hegel's theory of religion.

Harris, Errol E., *An Interpretation of the Logic of Hegel*, Lanham: University Press of America, 1983.

This book is much more than just an "introduction" to Hegel's Logic. It successfully attempts to show what the essence of Hegel's logic is in itself and apart from the rest of Hegelian philosophic system, and what the function of logic is within the context of that system. Hegel's logic is united with the rest of his philosophy so essentially that without it the entire system of necessity collapses. This is hardly the case with most other systems of philosophy.This is a highly valuable book for those who want to develop a good grasp of Hegel's logic—both graduate and undergraduate students and even the instructors will benefit from it.

Hyppolite, Jean, *Genèse et structure de la Phénoménologie de Hegel*, Paris: Aubier, 1946.

This is a veritable masterpiece among the commentaries on Hegel's Phenomenology, or on any other work, for that matter. The author has spared nothing to produce this monumental work, which fortunately has been finally translated into English. While giving excellent exposition of all the major structural components of the Phenomenology and lucidly tracing their genesis to earlier antecedents of Hegel's thought, the author never treats this work as if It were just another book by Hegel. Rather he treats it as expressing Hegel's entire philosophy at the first stage of its development – exactly as Hegel himself viewed it. The work bristles with original interpretations and brilliant insights into the very depths of Hegel's philosophy and it is to be highly recommended to all those who wish to develop a thorough grasp of this monumental work, *The Phenomenology of Spirit/Mind*, the work of a true genius.

Lauer, Quentin, *Hegel's Concept of God*, Albany : State University of New York Press, 1982.

The book begins by showing that there are several conflicting interpretations of what Hegel means by the concept of God. There are those who like Fackenheim assert that Hegel is affirming a God that is transcendent to the world in a traditional Judeo-Christian sense. Then there are those, at the other extreme of the spectrum of opinions, who like Kojève hold that Hegel's God is nothing more than human spirit in both individual and social dimensions. Finally, there are those who take an intermediate position, holding that Hegel's God is essentially a theistic God conceived in a highly distorted way and thus in constant danger of being explained away. Lauer's own thesis in the matter – situated somewhere in the middle of the spectrum – is that Hegel's God is to be conceived dialectically, that is, as both immanent and transcendent, infinite and finite, free and determined in His actions, etc. etc.. Lauer does not see any insuperable conflict between the Hegelian and the Thomistic God. If anything, Hegel's God might cautiously be considered an improvement over St. Thomas's God. The principal merit of the book is that it attempts to show that the God is the central concept of Hegelian system, making thus his philosophy of necessity into a religion, as Hegel himself says. The book is bound to be an indispensable aid to those who seriously try to fathom Hegel's Doctrine of God, the nature of religion, and of philosophy itself.

Löwith, Karl, *From Hegel to Nietzsche : The Revolution in Nineteenth Century Thought*, trans. by E. E. Green, New York: Holt, 1964.

19th century philosophy, which in substance is German philosophy, is shown in this book to have unfolded itself "in the shadow of Hegel." Unable to contain many conflicting tendencies of their age within a powerful system, as Hegel had done, different thinkers developed different tendencies separately and in isolation from each other. Their minds were not powerful enough to grasp conflicting aspects of the intellectual, religious, political, and social reality as a systematic and dialectical whole, and thus they went into different directions. But whatever they did, whether rebelling against Hegel's view of God and Christian religion, or revolting against Hegel's conception of the State, or attempting new approaches to philosophy, they did all these things under the inescapable influence of Hegel and, in essence, merely elaborated further the themes which Hegel himself had broached and pursued the tendencies which Hegel himself had followed. The Hegelian system is thus perceived as having contained within itself the seeds of its own destruction. The book is quite readable and is usually found very helpful by students attempting to develop a deeper grasp of 19th century philosophy.

Marcuse, Herbert, *Reason and Revolution: Hegel and the Rise of Social Theory*, New York: Humanities, 1954.

A valuable book by an outstanding Hegel scholar of leftist tendencies. It shows the impact of Hegel's *Philosophy of Right* and of his *Philosophy of History* on Marx, Engels, and other last century thinkers and thus on the development of social and economic theory. Economic interpretation of social institutions and cultural values, which is today a commonplace in the Western society, is unthinkable without Marx and ultimately without Hegel. Can be profitably used by undergraduates studying 19th century thought.

A 9-HOUR MODULE COURSE IN HEGEL'S PHILOSOPHY

lst Class - General Introduction to 19th Century Philosophy.

Romanticism and German Philosophical Idealism.
Fichte's Kant Critique
Fichte's Dialectical Method
Fichte's System of Subjective Idealism
Fichte's Impact on Schelling & Hegel

2nd Class - Schelling:

Schelling's Fichte Critique
Schelling's Own Dialectical Method
Schelling's System of Objective Idealism
a) The Identity Philosophy
b) The Positive Philosophy
Schelling's Impact on Hegel & Posterity

3rd Class - Hegel:

Hegel's Fichte & Schelling Critique
Hegel's Own Dialectical Method
Hegel's System of Absolute Idealism, as formulated in his *Encyclopaedia of Philosophical Sciences*

4th Class - Hegel's Logic:

a) The Doctrine of Being
b) The Doctrine of Essence
c) The Doctrine of Concept
Hegel's Philosophy of Nature – Rudiments

5th Class - Hegel's Philosophy of Spirit:

Brief Introduction to Philosophy of History: Rectilinear, Goal-Oriented
a) Oriental Civilization
b) Greco-Roman Civilization
c) Germanic-Christian Civilization

6th Class - Hegel: Political Philosophy (from *Philosophy of Right*)

a) The Purpose of Political Philosophy
b) The Limits of Political Philosophy
c) The Structure & Function of Hegelian State
d) Hegel's View of Morality & Ethics

7th Class - Hegel: Philosophy of Art (from his Introduction to *Philosophy of Art*)

a) Symbolic Art
b) Classical Art
c) Romantic Art

8th Class - Hegel: Philosophy of Religion (from Introduction to *Philosophy of Religion*)

a) The Essence of Religion
b) Religion and Philosophy—identical.
c) Natural Religion & Religion of Art
d) The Revealed Religion (from 3rd Part of *Philosophy of Religion*)

9th Class - Hegel: Phenomenology of Spirit: A Highlight or Two

Hegel's Impact on 19th & 20th Century Philosophy
Conclusion.

Thirteen

Classic Modern Skepticism and Atheism

Donald Jarnevic

Eighteenth-Century Deistic, Sceptical, and Atheistic Philosophy

A. David Hume

Dialogues Concerning Natural Religion (1779), edited by Norman Kemp Smith. Indianapolis: The Bobbs-Merrill Company, Inc., 1947.

Hume's great classic criticizing the argument from design as well as a version of the cosmological argument for the existence of God.

Secondary Sources

J. C. A. Gaskin, *Hume's Philosophy of Religion*. New York: Barnes and Noble, 1978.

The author's purpose is "to bring Hume's various accounts of religion into a coherent picture in which it can be seen that his failure to find any convincing reasons for religious belief in the arguments of natural religion leads him first to consider religion's foundation in revelation, then to consider its possible status as a 'natural instinct,' and finally to search for its causes in human nature." He tries to show that "Hume's conclusions about religion form a coherent whole and that his critique moves steadily towards one crucial conclusion. . . . that natural order may possibly take its origin from an intelligent being, but if it does then that being has no moral claim upon or interest in mankind."

Norman Kemp Smith, *The Philosophy of David Hume: A Critical Study of Its Origins and Central Doctrines*. London: Macmillan and Company, Limited, 1949.

An important standard work which examines the influences which helped shape Hume's philosophy and which presents both a preliminary simplified statement and a detailed consideration of Hume's central doctrines.

G. P. Morice, ed., *David Hume's Bicentenary Papers*. Edinburgh: At the University Press, 1977.

Contains a paper by Ernest C. Mossner, "Hume and the Legacy of the Dialogues," which attempts to "approach the *Dialogues* from the biographical point of view, together with a survey of its artistic structure, and . . . a modicum of philosophical analysis, seeking to determine whether a resolution may be found of the several disputed areas."

Stanley Tweyman, *Scepticism and Belief in Hume's Dialogues Concerning Natural Religion*. Dordrecht: Martinus Nijhoff Publishers, 1986.

An examination of the sections of the *Dialogues* concerned with the argument from design. Argues that belief in an intelligent designer of the world is akin to 'natural beliefs' in causality, physical objects, and a continuing self, and claims that the "mitigated sceptic's defense of the unknowability of the divine nature is. . . in accordance with Hume's view that whatever is believed naturally cannot be known or understood."

B. Denis Diderot

Interpreter of Nature: Selected Writings, translated by Jean Stewart and Jonathan Kemp, edited and with an introduction by Jonathan Kemp. New York: International Publishers, 1963.

A collection of Diderot's writings selected with a view to assisting the study of modern dialectical materialism and preceded by a polemical introductory essay which is decidedly Marxist in character.

Selected Writings, selected and edited, with an introduction and notes by Lester G. Crocker; translated by Derek Coltman. New York: The Macmillan Company, 1966.

A wide selection from Diderot's writings, chronologically arranged and including an early deistic work as well as later materialistic and atheistic essays and dialogues. Diderot is especially interesting because of his resistance to Newtonian mechanism and his search for a more organismic view of reality.

Secondary Sources

W. H. Barker, J. H. Brumfitt, R. A. Leigh, R. Shackleton, and S. S. B. Taylor, *The Age of the Enlightenment: Studies Presented to Theodore Besterman*. Edinburgh: Oliver and Boyd, 1967.

Studies by more than two dozen scholars focusing on Voltaire and his contemporaries as well as on the age of the Enlightenment.

Lester G. Crocker, *Diderot's Chaotic Order*. Princeton: Princeton University Press, 1974.

A synthetic presentation of Diderot's thought organized in the categories of cosmic order, aesthetics, morals, and politics.

John Hope Mason, *The Irresistible Diderot*. London: Quartet Books, 1982.

An introduction to the life and work of Diderot, followed by a selection of his writings organized in such categories as atheism, discovery, aesthetics, morality, and politics—each preceded by an introductory essay.

Aram Vartanian, *Diderot and Descartes: A Study of Scientific Naturalism in the Enlightenment*. Princeton: Princeton University Press, 1953.

A study which traces "the evolution of materialist science from its Cartesian sources to Diderot and his contemporaries."

C. Paul Henri Thiry, Baron d'Holbach

The System of Nature, or Laws of the Moral and Physical World (2 vols., 1770), with notes by Diderot; translated by H. D. Robinson. New York: Burt Franklin, 1970.

An interpretation of nature and of the human in terms of matter in motion. A consideration of the origin of our ideas concerning the divinity and of proofs for the existence of a Deity. A defense of the thesis that atheism is compatible with morality and a review of motives which lead to atheism.

Secondary Sources

Max Pearson Cushing, *Baron d'Holbach: A Study of Eighteenth-Century Radicalism in France*. New York: Burt Franklin, 1914; reprinted 1971.

A brief introduction to the man and his works with special emphasis on *Systeme de la Nature*. Includes a bibliography of editions of Holbach's works in chronological order.

Alan Charles Kors, *d'Holbach's Coterie: An Enlightenment in Paris*. Princeton: Princeton University Press, 1976.

A careful study of the philosophies, men of letters, and scientists who met at the homes of the Baron d'Holbach during the second half of the eighteenth century. A scholarly presentation of what the author calls "a contextual portrait and analysis of this coterie that should restore something of the genuine to our sense of its character and its clime." Offers a fresh interpretation of the *coterie holbachique*.

W. H. Wickwar, *Baron d'Holbach: A Prelude to the French Revolution*. London: George Allen and Unwin, Ltd., 1935.

A consideration of Holbach's life and work. Of particular interest are the sections dealing with his atheism, his condemnation of revealed religion as immoral, his explanation of its continued hold over the human mind, and what hopes he had of overthrowing it.

D. Voltaire, Francois Marie de Arouet

Philosophical Dictionary, 2 vols., translated with an introduction and glossary by Peter Gay; preface by André Maurois. New York: Basic Books, 1962.

Treatments, often polemical in nature, of philosophical, religious, and historical terms many of which are relevant for the general theme of science and religion.

Secondary Sources

H. T. Mason, *Pierre Bayle and Voltaire*. London: Oxford University Press, 1963.

Useful for understanding Voltaire's approach to biblical criticism, Christian beliefs, the problem of evil, atheism, and natural morality, as well as to proofs of the existence and attributes of God and the relation between faith and reason.

Ira Wade, *The Intellectual Development of Voltaire*. Princeton: Princeton University Press, 1969.

A study of the overall course of Voltaire's life as a thinker, which includes a treatment of his own philosophical activity as well as of his relation to other philosophers.

E. The French Enlightenment

J. H. Brumfitt, *The French Enlightenment*. London: Macmillan Press, Ltd., 1972.

A brief study of the sources and character of the French Enlightenment accompanied by a helpful bibliographical appendix.

Peter Gay, *The Party of Humanity: Essays in the French Enlightenment*. New York: Alfred A. Knopf, 1964.

Studies sympathetic to the Enlightenment, which are useful for acquiring a sense of Voltaire's *Philosophical Dictionary* as well as some grasp of the Enlightenment in general.

Ira O. Wade, *The Structure and Form of the French Enlightenment*, 2 vols. Princeton: Princeton University Press, 1977.

A large study of which the most relevant parts for the theme of science and religion include "Religion to Holbach and Helvetius," "Science to Buffon," and "Holbach, Voltaire, and the Debate on Atheism."

Peter Gay, *The Enlightenment: A Comprehensive Anthology*. New York: Simon and Schuster, 1973.

Excerpts of substantial length from the various important writings of the Enlightenment period.

Nineteenth-Century Materialism and Atheism.

A. Ludwig Feuerbach

The Essence of Christianity (1841), translated by George Eliot, introductory essay by Karl Barth, forward by H. Richard Niebuhr. New York: Harper & Row, Publishers, 1957.

A humanistic account of religion in general: consciousness of God is understood as the self-consciousness of the human and the Christian mysteries are interpreted in terms of human qualities and conditions. The introductory essay by Barth, which treats the development of Feuerbach's position, is worth reading in its own right.

Lectures on the Essence of Religion (1848-1849), translated by Ralph Manheim. New York: Harper & Row, Publishers, 1967.

A broader treatment of religion than his *The Essence of Christianity.* It also considers non-Christian religions and understands the basis of religion to be the human's feeling of dependence upon nature. The divine attributes are interpreted as attributes of nature and atheism is deemed a positive and affirmative view which restores to nature and humankind the dignity and life of which they have been despoiled by theism.

B. Karl Marx and Friedrich Engels

On Religion, reprinted from the edition of 1957 published by the Foreign Languages Publishing House, Moscow; introduction by Reinhold Niebuhr. New York: Schocken Books, Inc., 1964.

Selections from the writings of Marx and Engels which treat science and religion as opposed, affirm the human to be one with nature, and present a naturalistic account of the origin of Christianity. Sometimes more polemical than philosophical in tone. Since some of the selections are quite short, it may be desirable to supplement this collection with complete texts of such works as *Critique of Hegel's Philosophy of Right* and *On the Jewish Question*.

Secondary Sources

Richard T. DeGeorge, *Patterns of Soviet Thought: The Origins and Development of Dialectical and Historical Materialism*. Ann Arbor: The University of Michigan Press, 1966.

A good basic introduction to the philosophical background of Soviet philosophy, including Hegel, the Young Hegelians, Feuerbach, and Marx, and the subsequent development of Leninism and Soviet philosophy and ideology.

Richard T. DeGeorge and James P. Scanlan, eds. *Marxism and Religion in Eastern Europe: Papers Presented at the Banff International Slavic Conference, September 4-7, 1974.*

Topics explored include the diverse approaches to philosophy taken by contemporary Marxist theorists as well as relations between the Soviet state and both Catholic and Islamic believers.

Alasdair MacIntyre, *Marxism and Christianity*. New York: Schocken Books, 1968.

Considers some of the historical background of Marx's critique of religion and argues that Marxism, which is viewed as the historical successor of Christianity, shares "both the content and the functions of Christianity as an interpretation of human existence."

Tom Rockmore, William J. Gavin, James G. Colbert, & Thomas J. Blakeley, *Marxism and Alternatives: Towards the Conceptual Interaction Among Soviet Philosophy, Neo-Thomism, Pragmatism and Phenomenology*. Dordrecht, Holland: D. Reidel Publishing Company, 1981.

The subtitle aptly describes this work, which includes such chapters as "The Scientific-Technological Revolution," "Natural Law and the Common Good," "Science and Progress," and "Metaphenomenology."

John Somerville and Howard L. Parsons, eds., *Dialogues on the Philosophy of Marxism: From the Proceedings of the Society for the Philosophical Study of Dialectical Materialism*. Westport, Connecticut: Greenwood Press, 1974.

Papers on various aspects of Marxist philosophy, e.g., Marxism and philosophy of science, Marxism and humanism, Marxism's image of man.

Gustav Wetter, *Dialectical Materialism: A Historical and Systematic Survey of Philosophy in the Soviet Union*, translated by Peter Heath. New York: Frederick A. Praeger, publisher, 1958.

A more comprehensive exposition of the philosophical background and development of Marxism and Soviet theory.

Fourteen

Roots of Positivism: Comte, Mill, and Mach

Don H. Olive

Auguste Comte (1798-1857)

Comte, Auguste. *The Positive Philosophy*. Freely translated and condensed by Harriet Martineau. 2 vols. Third ed. London: Kegan Paul, Trench, Trubner, & Co., 1893.

This translation is a condensation of Comte's *Cours de philosophie positive*, 1830-1842, a *magnum opus* of 4700 pages in six volumes.

Vol. I: This volume consists of an Introduction in two chapters and five Books, each with multiple chapters. Each Book details Comte's review of "what has been effected in the Sciences" (p. 7) in order to make clear each science's relation to the positive system. For each science Comte set out the "methods and chief results" (p. 7) in order to establish the positive sciences of mathematics, astronomy, physics, chemistry, and biology as harbingers of and patterns for positive philosophy. The two chapters of the Introduction, in spite of Comte's diffuseness, set out the nature and importance of positive philosophy, as well as its structure built upon the filiation of the five positive sciences.

These two schematic and important chapters have been recently republished with a new introduction and a revised translation by Frederick Ferré in *Introduction to Positive Philosophy* (Hackett Publishing Company, Inc., 1988, 70 pp. Reprint edition.) In the first introductory chapter Comte sketched the advantages of a study of Positive Philosophy. He claimed that the study "affords the only rational means of exhibiting the logical laws of the human mind . . ." (p. 9), regenerates education, advances science by combining them, and "offers the only solid basis for that Social Reorganization which must succeed the critical condition in which the most civilized nations are now living" (p. 12). The second introductory chapter treated of the organization of the positive sciences, those sciences whose phenomena have already been shown to be subject to the invariable laws of nature. For Comte, each science is identified in terms of its phenomena and is ranked in terms of its dependency upon the principles of the preceding science. The highest level of generality is reached in positive philosophy, which partakes of the essential general properties of what Comte called "filiation." These properties are: (1) the arrangement rises spontaneously from the sciences themselves, (2) the arrangement conforms to the actual order of development of natural philosophy, (3) the arrangement indicates the relative perfection of the sciences, and (4) the arrangement sets the pattern for an entirely rational scientific education.

Vol. II: The second volume consists of Book VI of Comte's *Cours de philosophie positive*. It outlines in some detail the new science Comte viewed as the heart of positive philosophy, i.e. "Social Physics," or sociology. In addition to spelling out the lines of the new science, Comte examined the history of mankind under the rubric of the three stages: theological, metaphysical, and positive. The last is marked by the recognition of the natural laws of social organization.

Comte concluded this Book with an estimate of the final actions (benefits) of positive philosophy.

Comte, Auguste. *System of Positive Polity: Treatise on Sociology, Instituting the Religion of Humanity.* 4 vols. Trans. by John Henry Bridges. New York: Burt Franklin, 1966.

The first volume in this series consists of two treatises: *The General View of Positivism* and *Introductory Principles*. The subtitle of the first treatise is "Summary Exposition of the System of Thought and Life Adapted to the Great Western Republic, formed of the Five Advanced Nations, the French, Italian, Spanish, British and German, which, since the time of Charlemagne, have always constituted a Political Whole." Comte argued that positivistic philosophy offers a systematic view of human life as a basis for modifying its imperfections. Even though the social organization of the world operates by laws of nature, for the most part, it can be modified to the benefit of society, Humanity, and its organic parts, humans. Comte examined the modifications expected with respect to the working classes, women, and art. He concluded with a discussion of the religion of humanity.

Humanity is the Great Being which consecrates Science. Comte set out the interrelations and lines of a missionary religion including a Positive Council, made up first of representatives of the Five Western Nations. Comte envisioned the religion as then spreading to the remaining portions of the world. Comte concluded that "after having thus exercised our powers to the full, and having given a charm and sacredness to our temporary life, we shall at least be for ever incorporated into the Supreme Being, of whose life all noble natures are necessarily partakers."

The second treatise sets out the preliminary considerations of the religion of humanity as it has come to expression in society. As religion consists of doctrine, life, and worship, so the science of society is presented as sociology, sociocracy, and sociolatry (p. 327). Comte explored the grounds of the Philosophy of Society in the analytic and synthetic aspects of natural philosophy. The analytic aspect is cosmology, which includes mathematics, astronomy, physics, and chemistry. The synthetic aspect is biology, including topics of psychology, a science Comte refused to recognize as positivistic.

Vol. II sets out Comte's positive doctrine, sociology, "a last class of natural laws, less obvious than any of the others, although they even more nearly concern us" (p. 48). Under these laws men feel how bound up each is with his contemporaries and predecessors until "the entire system of Positive Belief points to the existence of a single dominant Power; whose real and incontestable attributes appeal directly to the Affections, in no less measure than they appeal to the Intellect" (p. 47). They appeal to the affections precisely because they form the subjective synthesis which unifies all men in Humanity, the object of religion. Comte claimed that this synthesis is the "only one that is complete and durable; for it is the only one in true conformity with our nature" (p. 58). Having given this general theory of religion as the basis for sociology, Comte then discussed society under topics of property, family, language, organization, social existence, and social variation.

Vol. III is Comte's attempt to give historical illustrations of his ideas concerning sociology. And Vol. IV presents the practical application of them.

Comte, Auguste. *The Catechism of Positivism, or Summary Exposition of the Universal Religion.* Trans. Richard Congreve,

London, 1858. This work is found in Vol. XI of the *Oeuvres d'Auguste Comte*. Paris, Ernest Leroux, 1970.

Among other dynamics of the religion of humanity, Comte emphasized the power of the positivistic liturgical calendar and the use of the 150 volumes of the Positivist Library.

Comte, Auguste. *Auguste Comte and Positivism: The Essential Writings*. Ed. with intro. by Gertrud Lenzer. Chicago: University of Chicago Press, 1975.

In addition to an excellent introductory essay entitled, "Auguste Comte and Modern Positivism," this volume contains the most extensive selections from the writings of Comte available. Materials range from early essays on reorganizing society to the last writings concerning religion.

Secondary Works

Caird, Edward. *The Social Philosophy and Religion of Comte*. Glasgow: James Maclehose & Sons, 1885.

This work is primarily a critique of Comte's religion. Caird argued that Comte's God, Humanity, is an incoherent subjective synthesis. Because it is relative, it cannot serve as the object of worship, although it may be sufficient for a moral ideal.

Hawkins, Richmond Laurin. *Auguste Comte and the United States (1816-1853)*. Cambridge: Harvard University Press, 1936.

Hawkins proposed in this work to chronicle the history of the reception of Comte's doctrines in the United States up to the publication of Martineau's translation in late 1853. He identified three moments in this history: scattered articles and notices early on, the anti-positivistic writings of George Frederick Holmes from 1851-54, and the efforts after 1853 of Henry Edger to establish the Religion of Humanity in the village Modern Times, Long Island.

Schneider, Robert Edward. *Positivism in the United States: The Apostleship of Henry Edger.* Republica Argentina: Rosario, 1946.

A study of Henry Edger's attempt at establishing positivism in the United States.

Standley, Arline Reilein. *Auguste Comte.* Boston: Twayne Publishers, 1981.

This work professes to be an attempt to "sort out what Comte really said and what he was really significant for," directed to the nonspecialist who is confused by varying statements concerning positivism and Comte. Standley aimed to outline the evolution of Comte's thought, to explicate his major works, to explore his basic assumptions, and to demonstrate some of the ways in which Comte's ideas were influential. Of particular interest is Standley's discussion of positive aesthetics, a subject which was given increasing attention by Comte in working out the implications of his religion of humanity.

Whittaker, Thomas. *Comte and Mill.* London: Archibald Constable & Co., Ltd., 1908.

This older comparative study of Comte and Mill still provides excellent insights into each thinker. Whittaker focused on central ideas in each and those ideas upon which they agreed.

John Stuart Mill (1806-1873)

Mill, John Stuart. *Collected Works.* 21 vols. Ed. John M. Robson. Toronto: University of Toronto Press, 1961-1981.

MacMinn, N., J. R. Hainds, and J. M. McCrimmon (eds.). *Bibliography of the Published Writings of John Stuart Mill.*

Evanston: Northwestern University Press, 1945. [Generally cited as reproducing Mill's own incomplete list.]

Mill, John Stuart. *A System of Logic.* Vols. VII and VIII of *Collected Works*. Toronto: University of Toronto Press, 1973.

This work, although designated by R. P. Anschutz as "by far the most important of [Mill's] philosophical books" (*Critical Essays* 50), is primarily noteworthy for its defense of induction and experimental inquiry. Induction has two questions: "how to ascertain the laws of nature [expressions of the uniformities which exist among natural phenomena]; and how to follow them into their results [a web which consists of the separate rules or modes of taking place which different natural phenomena have]" (p. 318). The rules of experimental inquiry in Book III, Chapters 8-10, were Mill's "contrivances for unraveling the web." Bertrand Russell wrote of this work, "Everything that Mill has to say in his *Logic* about matters other than inductive inference is perfunctory and conventional" (*Critical Essays 2).*

Mill, John Stuart. *Autobiography and Literary Essays.* Vol. I of *Collected Works.* Toronto: University of Toronto Press, 1981.

Mill set before the reader three reasons for the posthumously published *Autobiography.* He wrote: "I have thought that . . . it may be useful that there should be some record of an education which was unusual and remarkable, and which . . . has proved how much more than is commonly supposed may be taught, and well taught in those early years which . . . are little better than wasted. It has also seemed to me that . . . there may be somewhat both of interest and of benefit in noting the successive phases of any mind which was always pressing forward. . . . But a motive which weighs more with me than either of these, is a desire to make acknowledgment of the debts which my intellectual and moral development owes to other persons" (p. 5). This work is a storehouse of information concerning Mill and his interaction with the intellectual circles of his day. The "Bibliographic Index of Persons and Works Cited" occupies some 117 pages. An extensive topic index allows access to various statements Mill made with respect to almost any topic.

Mill, John Stuart. *The Positive Philosophy of Auguste Comte.* New York: H. Holt, 1887.

This work is a critical summary of Comte's positive philosophy as expressed in the *Cours de philosophie positive.* Mill testified to substantial agreement with this "sound view of philosophy, with a few capital errors" (p. 6). At the same time he deemed Comte's speculations concerning the positive polity "false and misleading" (p. 6). Indeed, in *On Liberty* Mill characterized Comte's later work as aiming "at establishing a despotism of society over the individual, surpassing anything contemplated in the political ideal of the most rigid disciplinarian among the ancient philosophers" (pp. 18-19).

Mill summed up Comte's positive philosophy: "We have no knowledge of anything but Phenomena; and our knowledge of phenomena is relative, not absolute. We know not the essence, nor the real mode of production, of any fact, but only its relations to other facts in the way of succession or of similitude. These relations are constant; that is, always the same in the same circumstances. The constant resemblances which link phenomena together, and the constant sequences which unite them as antecedent and consequent, are termed their laws. The laws of phenomena are all we know respecting them. Their essential nature, and their ultimate causes, either efficient or final, are unknown and inscrutable to us" (pp. 7-8).

Mill, John Stuart. *An Examination of Sir William Hamilton's Philosophy and of the Principal Philosophical Questions Discussed in his Writings.* Vol. IX of *Collected Works.* Toronto: University of Toronto Press, 1979.

Mill gave a lengthy explication of and attack upon Hamilton's intuitionist philosophy because he regarded the doctrine that we have intuitive and infallible knowledge of the principles governing either ourselves or the outside world as "the great intellectual support of false doctrines and bad institutions." Mill characterized intuitionism as "an instrument devised for consecrating all deep seated prejudices" (*Autobiography* 134).

Chapter VII is an intense attack upon equivocity concerning God's attributes, a position taken by Henry Mansel, Hamilton's chief disciple at Oxford. Mill's famous statement followed: "If, instead of the 'glad tidings' that there exists a Being in whom all the excellences which the highest human mind can conceive, exist in a degree inconceivable to us, I am informed that the world is ruled by a being whose attributes are infinite, but what they are we cannot learn . . . ; convince me of it, and I will bear my fate as I may. But when I am told that I must believe this, and at the same time call this being by the names which express and affirm the highest human morality, I say in plain terms that I will not. Whatever power such a being may have over me, there is one thing which he shall not do: he shall not compel me to worship him. I will call no being good, who is not what I mean when I apply that epithet to my fellow-creatures; and if such a being can sentence me to hell for not so calling him, to hell I will go" (p. 103).

Mill, John Stuart. *Three Essays on Religion.* In *The Philosophy of John Stuart Mill: Ethical, Political and Religious.* Ed. by Marshall Cohen. New York: The Modern Library, 1961.

The three essays are titled "Nature," "Utility of Religion," and "Theism." Although all these essays were published posthumously in 1874, the first two were composed during the period between 1850 and 1858, to which belongs also the composition of *On Liberty* and *Utilitarianism*. "Theism" was written much later and little revised.

Mill argued that nature has two principle meanings. It can mean either the entire system of things or things as they would be without human intervention. Neither meaning, for Mill, provides warrant for determining the course of man's life upon the basis of nature. He concluded that whatever good nature brings to men "is mostly the result of their own exertions. Whatsoever, in nature, gives indication of beneficent design, proves this beneficence to be armed only with limited power; and the duty of man is to co-operate with the beneficent powers, not by imitating but by perpetually striving to amend the course of nature – and bringing that part of it over which we can exercise control, more nearly into conformity with a high standard of justice and goodness" (pp. 487-88).

The utility of religion can no longer be found in the supernatural sanction of social morality for Mill. For the individual, the assimilation of God as an abstract moral perfection to a revealed God of nature disqualifies it. Mill argued that the worship of a Deity of such an assimilation "becomes the bowing down to a gigantic image of something not fit for us to imitate. It is the worship of power only" (p. 518).

Despite these strong statements concerning the disutility of religion, Mill in "Theism" announced to the chagrin of many of his followers that religion serves as the basis of hope, a positive component in a successful life. Some design in nature (the eye appears to have been made for seeing) allows for the hypothesis of a deity limited in power and knowledge. Such a nonabsolute deity leaves room for a belief in objective immortality, although it certainly does not mandate it.

Mill, John Stuart. *On Liberty*. In *John Stuart Mill: A Selection of His Works*. Ed. John M. Robson. Toronto: Macmillan of Canada, 1966.

This landmark essay on the liberty (autonomy) of the individual is in five chapters. Mill's thesis set out in Chapter I is "that the only purpose for which power can be rightfully exercised over any member of a civilized community, against his will, is to prevent harm to others. His own good, either physical or moral, is not a sufficient warrant. . . . The only part of the conduct of anyone, for which he is amenable to society, is that which concerns others. In the part which merely concerns himself, his independence is, of right, absolute. Over himself, over his own body and mind, the individual is sovereign" (p. 14). Upon the assumption that all human apprehensions of truth are finite and fallible, Mill argued for liberty as the ultimate prerogative of the individual over against all authorities: religion, morality, government, public opinion, etc. Only by exercising this prerogative can man develop the social part of his nature.

Mill, John Stuart. *Utilitarianism*. In *John Stuart Mill: A Selection of His Works*. Ed. John M. Robson. Toronto: Macmillan of Canada, 1966.

In this important essay Mill proposed that the utilitarian hedonistic calculus be modified to include the qualitative distinction between higher and lower pleasures, a distinction he regarded as setting man off from other animals. What is higher is decided, according to Mill, upon the basis of human experience: the higher of two pleasures is that which "all or almost all who have experience of both give a decided preference" (p. 159). Mill claimed that the ultimate sanction of the principle of utility is no different from the sanction of other systems of morality, even if, as was his conviction, "moral associations . . . are wholly of artificial creation" (p. 187). After discussion of what sort of proof the principle of utility is susceptible – anything is desirable in that people do actually desire it (p. 192) – Mill examined the connection between justice and utility.

Mill, John Stuart. *The Subjection of Women.* In *John Stuart Mill: A Selection of His Works*. Ed. John M. Robson. Toronto: Macmillan of Canada, 1966.

Mill's thesis in this essay was "that the principle which regulates the existing social relations between the two sexes – the legal subordination of one sex to the other – is wrong in itself, and now one of the chief hindrances to human improvement; and that it ought to be replaced by a principle of perfect equality, admitting no power or privilege on the one side, nor disability on the other" (p. 358). Mill contended that emotion rather than reason is behind the opposition to sexual equality seen in the history of male domination. He further argued that sexual subordination is not natural but social, and as social is unjustified and unjustifiable.

Secondary Works

August, Eugene. *John Stuart Mill: A Mind at Large*. New York: Charles Scribner's Sons, 1975.

This work provides a topical and biographical study of Mill and his ideas from a literary point of view.

Douglas, Charles. *John Stuart Mill.* Reprint edition. Edinburgh: William Blackwood and Sons, 1895.

An older study of Mill, but particularly useful in examining Mill's relationship to positivism and its ideas.

Ryan, Alan. *John Stuart Mill.* New York: Pantheon Books, 1970.

Ryan aims to present John Stuart Mill as the author of a philosophical system called "inductivism." He builds upon Mill's idea of two logical systems: the *a priori* and the experiential.

Schneewind, J. B. (ed.). *Mill: A Collection of Critical Essays.* Notre Dame: University of Notre Dame Press, 1969.

A valuable collection of critical studies of Mill.

Whittaker, Thomas. *Comte and Mill.* London: Archibald Constable & Co., Ltd., 1908.

An older comparative, sympathetic study of Comte and Mill. Whittaker especially focuses upon the religious thought of both thinkers.

Ernst Mach (1838-1916)

Mach, Ernst. *The Science of Mechanics: A Critical and Historical Account of Its Development.* Trans. Thomas J. McCormack. Intro. Karl Menger. LaSalle, IL: Open Court Publishing Company, 1960.

Mach in this work offered not only a study of mechanics, static and dynamic, but also what he called the formal development of mechanics. Mach claimed that once the chief facts of a physical science have been fixed by observations, a period of deductive development transpires in which "the facts are reproducible in the mind without constant recourse to observation" (p. 516). In this period principles and theorems are used to express the more elementary facts and the more complex facts, respectively. This period is followed by the science's formal development where "it is sought to put in a clear compendious form, or *system*, the facts to be reproduced, so that each can be reached and mentally pictured with the *least intellectual effort*" (p. 516).

Mach argued that the prejudice that based philosophy and science on theology was only little by little erased and is not to be counted against the great physicists. They were men of stupendous intellect but caught in the contracted horizon of their age (p. 546). Consonant with his view that science is the act of "least intellectual effort" he foresaw the day when scientists would approach to that "ideal of a unified view of the world which is alone compatible with the economy of a sound mind" (p. 560). Building upon a sensationist epistemology, Mach affirmed: "It is the object of science to replace, or *save*, experiences, by the reproduction and anticipation of facts in thought. Memory is handier than experience, and often answers the same purpose. This economical office of science, which fills its whole life, is apparent at first glance; and with its full recognition all mysticism in science disappears" (p. 577).

Mach further explored the implications of this economical view of science as it relates to language (p. 578), sensations (p. 579), causality (pp. 580-581), mathematics and method (pp. 582-586), and the physiological beginning point of physics (pp. 596-615). This last discussion led him to the position "that a real *economy* of scientific thought cannot be attained by mechanical hypotheses" (p. 599), even though many circumstances made it a tool whereby less known phenomena were explainable by better known mechanical events (p. 600).

Mach, Ernst. *The Analysis of Sensations and the Relation of the Physical to the Psychical*. Trans. C. M. Williams. Intro. Thomas S. Szasz. New York: Dover Publications, Inc., 1959.

This work in early psychology grew out of Mach's disinclination to reduce all science to physics, inasmuch as physics is "but a portion of a *larger* collective body of knowledge, and that it is unable, with its limited intellectual implements, created for limited and special purposes, to exhaust all the subject-matter in question" (p. 1). Thus, Mach set before the reader his analysis of sensations, providing an "antimetaphysical" description of mind, a description in which "a very widespread prejudice is removed. . . . There is no rift between the psychical and the physical, no inside and outside, no 'sensation' to which an external 'thing,' different from sensation corresponds. There is but one kind of elements, out of which this supposed inside and outside are formed – elements which are themselves inside or outside, according to the aspect in which, for the time being, they are viewed" (p. 310).

Mach, Ernst. *Principles of Physical Optics*. New York: Dover Publications, Inc., [n.d.]. Available only on microfilm.

Mach, Ernst. *Space and Geometry, in the Light of Physiological, Psychological and Physical Inquiry*. Chicago: Open Court Publishing Co., 1906.

Mach argued here as elsewhere that space and time are sensations, along with color, temperature, etc. This led Einstein to affirm that "it is not improbable that Mach would have discovered the theory of relativity, if, at the time when his mind was still young and susceptible, the problem of the constancy of the speed of light had been discussed among physicists" (P. A. Schilpp [ed.]. *Albert Einstein: Philosopher-Scientist*. New York: Tudor Publishing Co., 1951, pp. 271-272).

Mach, Ernst. "Newton's Views of Time, Space, and Motion." In H. Feigl and M. Brodbeck (eds.). *Readings in the Philosophy of Science*. New York: Appleton-Century-Crofts, Inc., 1955.

In this work Mach challenged the prominent view associated with Newtonian physics that the proper aim of science is to produce "objective descriptions" of nature and to formulate these descriptions economically by theories which are "true."

Secondary Works

Ayer, A. J. *Logical Positivism*. 1959. Provides an introduction to and a historical sketch of Ernst Mach.

Carus, Paul. "Professor Mach's Philosophy." *Monist*. 16 (1906), 331-356. Carus principally criticizes Mach's sensationism as being no more than noting the subjectivity of the subjective in experience.

______. "Professor Mach's Philosophy and His Work." *Monist. 21* (1911), 19-42. A survey of Mach's philosophy of science.

Frank, P. "Einstein, Mach, and Logical Positivism." In P. A. Schilpp (ed.). *Albert Einstein: Philosopher-Scientist.* New York: Tudor Publishing Co., 1951. Explores Mach's influence upon Einstein.

______. *Modern Science and Its Philosophy*. New York: George Braziller, 1955.

Mises, R. von. *Positivism: A Study in Human Understanding.* New York: George Braziller, Inc., 1956.

Fifteen

Modern Controversies: Geology and Religion

J. A. Colombo

Primary Sources

Buckland, William

"Reliquiae Diluvianae," *Quarterly Review*, 2 (1809):138-65.

Vindiciae Geologicae, or the connection of geology with religion explained. Oxford, 1820.

Reliquiae Diluvianae, or observations on the organic remains contained in caves, fissures and diluvial gravel, and other geological phenomena, attesting the action of a universal deluge. 2nd ed., London, 1824.

Geology and Mineralogy considered with reference to Natural Theology. 2 vols. 2nd ed. London, 1837.

Burnet, Thomas

Sacred Theory of the Earth, 2 vols., 6th ed., London, 1690. Reprinted with an introduction by Basil Wiley. London: Centaur Press, 1962.

Chambers, Robert

Vestiges of the Natural History of Creation, 4th ed. London, 1844. Reprinted with an introduction by Sir Gavin de Beer. Leicester: University Press, 1969.

Explanations: A Sequel to the Vestiges, London, 1846.

Conybeare, William Daniel

"On Mr Lyell's Principles of Geology," *Philosophical Magazine*, 8 (1830): 215-219.

"A critique of uniformitarian geology: a letter from W. D. Conybeare to Charles Lyell, 1841," M. J. S. Rudwick, in *Proceedings of the American Philosophy Society* 111 (1967): 272-81.

Cuvier, Georges Baron

Lessons in Comparative Anatomy, 2 vols., London, 1802.

Essay on the Theory of the Earth, 2nd ed., Edinburgh, 1815.

Deluc, J.A.

"Letters to Dr. James Hutton, F.R.S. Ed., on his theory of the earth," *Monthly Review* 2 (1790): 206-27 and 582-601; 3 (1790): 573-86; 4 (1791): 564-85.

An Elementary Treatise on Geology, Trans. Henry de la Fite, London, 1809.

Fleming, John

"The Geological Deluge, as Interpreted by Bacon, Cuvier and Professor Buckland, Inconsistent with the Testimony of Moses and the Phenomena of Nature," *Edinburgh Philosophical Journal* 14 (1826): 205-39.

Hutton, James

"Theory of the Earth; or An Investigation of the Laws Observable in the Composition, Dissolution, and Restoration of Land Upon the Globe," *Transactions of the Royal Society of Edinburgh*, 1 (1788): 209-304.

Theory of the Earth with Proofs and Illustrations, 2 vols., Edinburgh, 1795.

Jameson, Robert

A System of Mineralogy, 3 vols., Edinburgh, 1804-1808.

Kirwan, Richard

Geological Essays, London, 1799.

Lyell, Sir Charles

Principles of Geology, 4 vols., 3 ed., London, 1834.

Lectures on Geology Delivered at the Broadway Tabernacle in the City of New York, New York, 1842.

"Anniversary Address of the President," *Quarterly Journal of the Geological Society of London*, 6 (1850): xxvii-lxvi.

"The Theory of the Successive Geological Development of Plants, from the Earliest Periods to Our Own Time, as Deduced from Geological Evidence," *Edinburgh New Philosophical Journal*, 51 (1851): 213-26.

"The Theory of Successive Development in the Scale of Being both Animal and Vegetable, from the Earliest Periods to Our Own Time, as Deducted from Paleontological Evidence," *Edinburgh New Philosophical Journal*, 51 (1851): 1-31.

"Anniversary Address of the President," *Quarterly Journal of the Geological Society of London*, 7 (1851): xxxii-lxxi.

The Antiquity of Man, London, 1863.

Miller, Hugh

The Footprints of the Creator; or, The Asterolepis of Stromness, Boston, 1850.

The Testimony of the Rocks; or Geology in its Bearings on the Two Theologies, Natural and Revealed, Boston, 1857.

Playfair, John

Illustrations of the Huttonian Theory of the Earth, Edinburgh, 1802.

Sedgwick, Adam

"Presidential Address," *Proceedings of the Geological Society of London* 1 (1831): 281-316.

"Vestiges of the Natural History of Creation," *Edinburgh Review* 82 (1845): 1-85. Discourse on the Studies of the University of Cambridge, 5th ed., London, 1850.

Smith, William

Strata Identified by Organized Fossils. London, 1816.

Stratigraphal System of Organized Fossils, London, 1817.

Townsend, Joseph

The Character of Moses Established for Veracity as a Historian Recording Events from the Creation to the Deluge, Bath, 1813.

Whewell, William

"Lyell's *Principles of Geology*, Vol. I.," *British Critic* 9 (1831): 180-206.

"Lyell's *Principles of Geology*, Vol. II," *Quarterly Review* 47 (1832): 103-32.

"Presidential Address," *Proceedings of the Geological Society of London* 3 (1838): 61-98.

History of the Inductive Sciences from the Earliest to the Present Time. 3 vols. New York, 1872.

Primary Sources in Anthologies

Albritton, Claude C., Ed. *Philosophy of Geohistory: 1785-1970*. Stroudsburg, Pennsylvania: Dowden, Hutchinson and Ross, 1975.

Relevant selections from Hutton, Playfair, Lyell and Whewell with an introductory essay by Stephen Toulmin entitled "The Discovery of Time."

Brooke, John Hedley, Hooykaas, R. and Lawless, Clive. *New Interactions between Theology and Natural Science*. Block 4 Units 9-11 of the series *Science and Belief: From Copernicus to Darwin*. Walton Hall, Milton Keynes, Great Britain: The Open University Press, 1974.

This rather extraordinary series prepared for the Open University presents an entire curriculum: a presentation of the specific subject-matter, correlated with specific readings available in other sources, with study-questions for the student. This particular block treats natural theology from Boyle to Paley and the Genesis and geology controversy. Along with the Goodman anthology, this is one of the most valuable items I have found with regards to curriculum development.

Goodman, D. C., Ed. *Science and Religious Belief 1600-1900: A Selection of Primary Sources*. Dorchester: Dorset Press, 1973.

An anthology of 26 texts which are specifically keyed to the Open University course "Science and Belief: From Copernicus to Darwin" (cf. above). First-rate anthology.

Mather, Kirtley F. and Mason, Shirley L. Eds. *A Source Book in Geology*. New York: McGraw-Hill Book Co., 1939.

A rather large (700 page) anthology from the period 1480 to 1920. About 120 writers are sampled here and a "Guide to the Subject Matter" (with entries such as "Vulcanism," "Stratigraphy, "Fossils" and "Life Development) is most helpful in directing one to relevant authors.

Russell, Colin Archibald. Ed. *Science and Religious Belief: A Selection of Recent Historical Studies*. London: University of London Press, 1973.

An excellent anthology of "classic" secondary texts correlated with the Open University course.

Secondary Sources

Bowler, Peter J. *Fossils and Progress: Paleontology and the Ideas of Progressive Evolution in the Nineteenth Century*. New York: Science History Publications, 1976.

Brooke, John Hedley. "The natural theology of the geologists: some theological strata," in *Images of the Earth: Essays in the History of the Environmental Sciences*. Eds. J. Jordanova and Roy S. Porter. Aberdeen, Scotland: Rainbow Enterprises, 1979.

While many secondary texts focus on the issue of "geology and Genesis," this article (as well as the Gillispie volume) seeks to explore the issue of "geology and the argument by design." A good article which with some background on the design argument shows the resiliency of this argument in the context of physical earth. Could be used for intro students.

Davies, Gordon L. *The Earth in Decay: A History of British Geomorphology 1578-1878*. London: Macdonald and Co., 1968.

While Gillispie's text (see below) focuses on the constitution of geology *vis a vis* religion with the emphasis on the latter, Davies does the same with the emphasis on the former. Lots of detail and as elegantly written as Gillispie. Given the detail, it might be for the advanced student.

Eiseley, Loren. *Darwin's Century*. Garden City, New York: Anchor Books, 1961.

Although not specifically on "geology and Genesis," Eiseley notes that the triumph of geological uniformitarianism was a necessary condition for Darwin's theory of natural selection and as such is treated in this context. Written in a rather breezy—and, to my mind, somewhat distracting—style, the book is readily accessible to the intro student.

Gillispie, Charles Coulston. *Genesis and Geology*. New York: Harper and Row, 1959.

Though almost three decades old, Gillispie's work remains the definitive study of the struggle to define the disciplinary parameters of geology against the "Mosaic geologists" and the geological proponents of a natural theology through the argument of design. Accessible to intro students, although the wealth of detail may be somewhat overwhelming.

_________. *The Edge of Objectivity*. Princeton: Princeton University Press, 1960.

Chapter 7 provides a concise précis of the larger work noted above.

Greene, Mott T. *Geology in the Nineteenth Century: Changing Views of a Changing World*. Ithaca: Cornell University Press, 1982.

A rather technical history. The first two chapters ("Hutton and Werner: First Principles" and "The Convergence of Geognosy and Geology, 1802-1818") are certainly relevant and accessible.

Haber, Francis C. *The Age of the World: Moses to Darwin*. Baltimore: The Johns Hopkins Press, 1959.

A rather detailed study of the geological controversy through the focus of the relation between biblical chronology and the rise of modern geological science. Particularly interesting is the review (pp. 38-60) of how "fossils" were regarded prior to the modern period. Quite accessible.

Hooykaas, R. *The Principle of Uniformity in Geology, Biology and Theology*. Leiden: E.J. Brill, 1963.

The substance of the text is exactly as indicated in the title. Quite readable, but probably the amount of detail restricts it to the major.

Moore, James R. "Geologists and Interpreters of Genesis in the Nineteenth Century," in *God and Nature: Historical Essays on the Encounter between Christianity and Science*. Edited by David Lindberg and Ronald Numbers. Berkeley: University of California Press, 1986.

Against the background of the Baconian compromise, the essay traces the emergence of a critical interpretation of Genesis. Focusing on the British Isles, this development is seen as an aspect of the broader attempt to establish professional boundaries between clergy and geological scientists. For the major.

Rudwick, Martin J. S. "The Shape and Meaning of Earth History," in *God and Nature: Historical Essays on the Encounter between Christianity and Science*. Edited by David Lindberg and Ronald Numbers. Berkeley: University of California Press, 1986.

A good essay whose thesis is that "specific episodes of conflict should be treated as stories of rival cosmologies" (297). Less attention is therefore given to the question of the "age of the earth," as distinct from the qualitative patterns attributed to the whole history of the earth. For the major.

__________. *The Meaning of Fossils: Episodes in the History of Paleontology*. London: Macdonald and Co., 1972.

A detailed and readable account of how fossils have been regarded. Rudwick especially focuses on the how the question of fossils conditioned the debate between uniformitarianism, catastrophism and progressivism.

Toulmin, Stephen and Goodfield, June. *The Discovery of Time*. Chicago: The University of Chicago Press, 1965.

The last volume of the series by Toulmin and Goodfield written for the Nuffield Foundation. The focus for the text is the process whereby living species and the planet acquired the rather elongated temporal horizons which we take for granted today. Chapter 7 deals specifically with the emergence of geology, although less attention is paid here than in the Gillispie pieces to the conflicts with the Christian religion. Quite accessible.

Williams, Arnold. *The Common Expositor: An Account on the Commentaries on Genesis 1527-1633*. Chapel Hill, North Carolina: The University of North Carolina Press, 1948.

Interesting background reading. What is not so startling is that in chapter 7 describing the "corruption of the world and the flood," virtually all the commentaries focus exclusively on the former. The latter is simply taken for granted as a dateable and universal event. As far as I can discern, the first writer for whom the flood itself becomes problematic is the Cartesian, Thomas Burnet. Accessible.

Sixteen

Roots of Religious Modernism: Schleiermacher

J. A. Colombo

Primary Sources

On Religion. Trans., with an introduction and notes by Terrence N. Tice. Richmond, Virginia: The John Knox Press, 1969.

On Religion. Trans. John Oman. New York: Harper and Brothers, 1958.

Oman's 1893 translation is still regarded as the "classic" one, although Tice's is more idiomatic. Speeches 2 and 5 most clearly convey the crux of Schleiermacher's position, are accessible to undergraduates, and should not be read in isolation from one another (*pace* Barth, Brunner and Gogarten). In the former, Schleiermacher seeks to argue that religion and religious experience is *sui generis* and thus differentiated from both "science" and "ethics." (Unfortunately, the fuller epistemological explication of this position remains untranslated in his *Dialektik*.) In the latter Speech, Schleiermacher deals with the plurality of religious traditions, the positivity of religion and the aporiae of "natural religion," suggesting that the eidetic analysis of Speech

2 is just that: an indeterminate abstraction whose concrete (and historical) embodiment is only to be found in specific religious traditions which materially are non-identical with one another.

Brief Outline on the Study of Theology. Trans., with an introduction and notes by Terence N. Tice. Richmond, Virginia: The John Knox Press, 1966.

As an exercise in "formal encyclopedia," Schleiermacher attempts to articulate the unity of theology as a "positive science" given the multiplicity of its various parts (i.e. philosophical, historical, practical theology each with their own subparts).

The Christian Faith. 2 vols. Various translators. Ed. H. R. Mackintosh and J.S. Stewart. Introduction to the Torchbook edition by Richard R. Niebuhr. New York: Harper & Row, 1963.

Schleiermacher's fullest exposition of the contents of the Christian faith. Organized into three parts which proceed from the most indeterminate to the determinate, it is a work best read as a whole, which many do not in fact do, but instead merely excerpt those propositions which deal only with "absolute dependence."

Hermeneutics: the Handwritten Manuscripts. Trans. James Duke and Jack Forstman. Ed. Heinz Kimmerle. Missoula, Montana: Scholars Press, 1979.

An important text for the history of hermeneutics, especially in understanding Dilthey.

On the Glaubenslehre: Two Letters to Dr. Lücke. Trans. James Duke and Francis Fiorenza. Chico, California: Scholars Press, 1981.

In these two letters to Lücke, Schleiermacher attempts to correct misinterpretations of *The Christian Faith*. An important text for understanding how Schleiermacher envisioned the task and limits of *Glaubenslehre*.

Christmas Eve: Dialogue on the Incarnation. Trans. Terence N. Tice. Richmond, Virginia: The John Knox Press, 1967.

Select Secondary Sources

Barth, Karl. *The Theology of Schleiermacher.* Trans. Geoffrey Bromiley. Ed. Dietrich Ritschl. Grand Rapids, Michigan: Eerdmans Publishing Co., 1982.

A wonderful exposition of the theology of Karl Barth even though the ostensible topic is Schleiermacher.

Gerrish, B.A. *A Prince of the Church: Schleiermacher and the Beginnings of Modern Theology*. Philadelphia: Fortress Press, 1984.

To a great extent, this book reflects a series of lectures given to a largely undergraduate audience at Valparaiso University. In my estimate, Gerrish is one of the most careful and subtle historical theologians of the 19th century. For the intro student.

__________. "Continuity and Change: Friedrich Schleiermacher on the Task of Theology," in *Tradition and the Modern World.* Chicago: University of Chicago Press, 1978.

For the major.

_________. "Schleiermacher and the Reformation: A Question of Doctrinal Development" and "Theology Within the Limits of Piety Alone: Schleiermacher and Calvin's Notion of God," in *The Old Protestantism and the New: Essays on the Reformation Heritage*. Chicago: University of Chicago Press, 1982.

For the major and professor.

Niebuhr, Richard R. *Schleiermacher on Christ and Religion*. New York: Scribner Books, 1967.

A readable and seminal work which broke the hegemony of the neo-orthodox interpretation-reception of Schleiermacher in the United States. For the major.

Redeker, Martin. *Schleiermacher: Life and Thought*. Trans. John Wallhauser. Philadelphia: Fortress Press, 1973.

A concise and accurate outline of Schleiermacher's thought which proceeds text by text. For the major.

Spiegler, Gerhard. *The Eternal Covenant: Schleiermacher's Experiment in Cultural Theology*. New York: Harper and Row, 1967.

The only full treatment of Schleiermacher's *Dialektik* in English. This provides a decent and competent access to material which is only in German. Yet Spiegler was a student of Charles Hartshorne and seems determined to find a di-polar theism in Schleiermacher. Having searched the *Dialektik*, I remain unconvinced even though I am sympathetic to Hartshorne. *À la* Schweitzer, Spiegler looks into the well for the historical Schleiermacher and finds proto-Hartshorne.

Tice, Terence N. *Schleiermacher Bibliography*. Princeton: Princeton Theological Seminary (Pamphlet No. 12), 1966.

A rather extensive bibliography of secondary sources until 1962 in German, English and French on all aspects of Schleiermacher's work.

Williams, Robert R. *Schleiermacher the Theologian: The Construction of the Doctrine of God*. Philadelphia: Fortress Press, 1978.

An excellent survey of Schleiermacher's understanding of God as refracted through the structure of the three forms of dogmatic assertions which lace the second and third parts of the *Glaubenslehre*. For the professor.

ADDENDUM

Part of my assigned task was also to come up with references for Wellhausen within the context of the rise of "higher criticism" of the Bible. I did not have much success in this regard. First, the work of Wellhausen itself must be taken within the context of a lengthy antecedent development, i.e., the emergence of a "historical consciousness" with regard to ancient documents which clustered around the elaboration of the categories of "myth," "saga," and "legend." Second, with regard to this wider development, I have found no sourcebook which documents through primary source material this development with respect to biblical criticism. Secondary materials are also scanty for this period and tend to begin with the work of Bousset, Gunkel, Dibelius and Bultmann in the twentieth century. Third, this state of affairs is not surprising inasmuch as the impetus towards the development of the category "myth" largely emerged outside the sphere of biblical criticism. Indeed, the category tends to be a nodal one which owes its existence in the sphere of biblical criticism to converging lines from a variety of disciplinary matrices, i.e., critical historiography, literary and aesthetic criticism, comparative religions, philosophy. With regard to this most general context, an excellent sourcebook is *The Rise of Modern Mythology 1680-1860*. Eds. Burton Feldman and Robert D. Richardson. Bloomington, Indiana: Indiana University Press, 1972. In addition this work (1) has lengthy introductions to each selection, (2) notes recent editions of each text and English translations when available, (3) cites recent secondary material and (4) has a lengthy, fuller annotated bibliography on "myth" at the end of the book.

Another critical piece would be Benjamin Jowett's contribution to the 1860 text *Essays and Reviews* – a text whose notoriety eclipsed Darwin's *Origin of the Species* for at least five years. Jowett, after reviewing the results of German "higher criticism" explicitly argues for that axiom which has been regulative for most subsequent biblical criticism: the text of the Bible is to be treated like any and every other text – a sort of hermeneutical principle of uniformity not unlike that which is contemporaneously emerging in geology and biology.

Seventeen

Darwin and Darwinism

Edward L. Schoen

Prior to Darwin, the mutability of species was considered by Montesquieu (1685-1755), Maupertuis (1698-1759) and Diderot (1713-1784). Both Erasmus Darwin (1731-1802) and Jean-Baptiste Lamarck (1744-1829), scientific predecessors of Charles Darwin (1809-1882), proposed theories of evolution in which they claimed that individuals possessed certain internal impulses for change. Lamarck thought that these impulses amounted to tendencies toward perfection and complexity and that inner feelings for change resulted from needs pressed upon individuals by their environments. Both Étienne Goeffroy Saint-Hilaire (1772-1844) and Baron Georges Cuvier (1769-1832) were important critics of the Lamarckian position. Cuvier suggested that natural history should be understood as a series of successive creations precipitated by periodic catastrophic disasters, such as the one recorded in the Noah story. After completing their own surveys of the evidence, both Charles Lyell (1797-1875) and James Hutton (1726-1797) pressed a uniformitarian doctrine, claiming that there was no evidence for periodic catastrophes. Instead, the principles of nature have operated uniformly throughout history. While Lyell admitted that a few species have become extinct and new ones occasionally have appeared, he thought that there was no evidence to support the claim that living things possess any inner impulses to progress. Furthermore, he could find no evidence of the gradual transition from one species to another.

Although Charles Darwin embraced the uniformitarianism of Lyell and Hutton, he turned to the work of Thomas Robert Malthus (1766-1834) as inspiration for his "survival of the fittest" motifs. While the position of Charles Bell (1774-1842) provides an excellent example of the sort of creationist biology against which Darwin was reacting, Sir Richard Owen (1804-1892) and Louis Agassiz (1807-1873) were among Darwin's most vigorous contemporary opponents. Among other names that fit prominently into the early creation-evolution story are John S. Henslow (1796-1861), who was Darwin's science teacher at Cambridge, William Buckland (1784-1856), Joseph Dalton Hooker (1817-1911), Robert Chambers (1802-1871), Georges Louis de Buffon (1707-1788), and Adam Sedgwick (1785-1873).

Abbreviated Bibliography:

Primary Sources

Agassiz, Louis, *Essays on Classification*, Edward Lurie, editor (Cambridge: Belknap Press, 1962), 268 pp.

Alland, Alexander, Jr., *Human Nature: Darwin's View* (New York: Columbia University Press, 1985), 242 pp.

24 page introductory overview of Darwin's thought on this topic. Easy reading. Remainder is easily read selections from Darwin's *Journal of Researches*, *The Descent of Man*, and *The Expressions of the Emotions in Man and Animals*.

Appleman, Philip, editor, *Darwin: A Norton Critical Edition* (New York: W. W. Norton and Company, 1970), 674 pp.

Selections from Darwin, Lyell, Bell, Hooker, Agassiz and 20th century figures concerning Darwin's relation to science, philosophy, theology, society and literature. By far the best single volume I have found for classroom use at nearly any level.

Barlow, Nora, editor, *Darwin and Henslow: The Growth of an Idea* (Berkeley: University of California Press, 1967), 251 pp.

Collection of letters with an introduction and appendices of related materials.

Bates, Marston and Humphrey, Philip S., *The Darwin Reader* (New York: Charles Scribner's Sons, 1956), 470 pp.

Includes good selections from Darwin, early and late.

Bixby, James Thompson, *The Ethics of Evolution: The Crisis in Morals Occasioned by the Doctrine of Development* (Boston: Small, Maynard and Company, 1900), 315 pp.

A critique of Spencer followed by a reconstruction of ethics on an evolutionary scientific basis.

Brunton, T. Lauder, *The Bible and Science* (London: Macmillan and Company, 1881), 415 pp.

An attempt to reconcile Biblical and Darwinian teachings.

Butler, Samuel, *Evolution Old and New* (London: Hardwicke and Bogue, 1879), 384 pp.

Describes Paley, Buffon, Erasmus Darwin, Lamarck, Spencer and Charles Darwin.

Chambers, Robert, *Vestiges of the Natural History of Creation* (New York: Humanities Press, 1969), 390 pp. Originally published in 1844.

Darwin, Charles, *The Descent of Man* (New York: Hurst and Company, 1874), 705 pp. Originally published in 1871.

Darwin, Charles, *The Expression of the Emotions in Man and Animals* (Chicago: University of Chicago Press, 1965), 372 pp.

Includes a treatment of guilt, despair and pride.

Darwin, Charles, *Journal of Researches* (New York: Hafner Publishing Company, 1952), 615 pp. Originally published in 1839.

Darwin, Charles, *The Origin of Species* (Cambridge: Harvard University Press, 1964), 502 pp. Originally published in 1859.

Darwin, Erasmus, *The Laws of Organic Life*, Volume I (New York: T & J Swords, 1796), 433 pp. Originally published in 1794.

Darwin, Erasmus, *The Laws of Organic Life*, Part II (Philadelphia: Thomas Dobson, 1797).

Hooker, Sir Joseph Dalton, *The Botany of the Antarctic Voyage* (London: Reeve, 1847-1860), four volumes.

Hull, David L., *Darwin and His Critics* (Chicago: University of Chicago Press, 1973), 473 pp.

About 80 pp. of commentary with the remainder being a collection of reviews by Darwin's contemporaries.

Huxley, Thomas H., *Darwiniana* (New York: D. Appleton and Company, 1897), 475 pp.

Discusses Darwin's theory and its critics.

Huxley, Thomas H., *Evolution and Ethics* (New York: D. Appleton and Company, 1918), 334 pp.

Huxley, Thomas H., *Man's Place in Nature* (New York: D. Appleton and Company, 1909), 329 pp.

Evolutionary themes with a final chapter on the Aryan question.

Huxley, Thomas H., *Method and Results* (New York: D. Appleton and Company, 1898), 430 pp.

Chapter 3 concerns the physical basis for life and Chapters 6-9 cover personal and social ethics.

Lamarck, Jean-Baptiste, *Hydrology* (Urbana: University of Illinois Press, 1964), 152 pp. Originally published in 1802.

Lamarck, Jean-Baptiste, *Zoological Philosophy*, Hugh Elliot, translator (Chicago: University of Chicago Press, 1984), 451 pp.

Includes several introductory essays.

Le Conte, Joseph, *Evolution and its Relation to Religious Thought* (New York: D. Appleton and Company 1889), 344 pp.

Chapters on man, nature, God, pantheism and the problem of evil.

Lyell, Sir Charles, *Principles of Geology*, fourth edition (London: J. Murray, 1835).

Patterson, Alexander, *The Other Side of Evolution: Its Effects and Fallacy* (Chicago: The Bible Institute Colportage Association, 1903), 153 pp.

Covers problems with evolutionary theory, its incompatibility with Scripture, and its deleterious effects.

Romanes, George John, *Mental Evolution in Animals* (New York: D. Appleton and Company, 1884), 411 pp.

Spencer, Herbert, *The Principles of Ethics* (New York: D. Appleton and Company, 1898), Volume I, 572 pp. Volume II, 505 pp.

Sutherland, Alexander, *The Origin and Growth of the Moral Instinct* (London: Longmans, Green and Company, 1898), Volume I, 461 pp., Volume II, 336 pp.

Detailed expansion on Darwin.

Wallace, Alfred Russel, *Contributions to the Theory of Natural Selection* (London: Macmillan and Company, 1870), 384 pp.

Wallace, Alfred Russel, *Miracles and Modern Spiritualism* (London: George Redway, 1896), 292 pp.

Response to Hume, "On Miracles." Scientific evidence is assembled supporting the existence of apparitions and phantasms. One chapter on the moral teachings of spiritualism. Easy reading.

Wallace, Alfred Russel, *Social Environment and Moral Progress* (London: Cassell and Company, 1913), 164 pp.

Morality, natural selection, heredity and environment. Chapters 13-16 concern evolutionary theory and ethics. Chapter 16 is entitled "Moral Progress through a New Form of Selection." Relatively easy reading.

Wallace, Alfred Russel, *The Wonderful Century* (London: G. Allen and Unwin, 1925), 527 pp.

Chapters describing evolution as well as notable failures of the science of his day. Includes a lamentation over the neglect of phrenology.

Washburn, Margaret Floy, *The Animal Mind* (New York: Macmillan, 1908), 330 pp.

An identification of mind in the natural order.

Secondary Sources

Barthelemy-Madaule, Madeleine, *Lamarck the Mythical Precursor: A Study of the Relations between Science and Ideology*, M. H. Shank, translator (Cambridge: MIT Press, 1982), 174 pp.

Bibby, Cyril, *The Essence of T. H. Huxley* (New York: St. Martin's Press, 1967), 246 pp.

Brief interpretive essays with selections from Huxley on various topics. Included are selections on agnosticism, evolution, ethics and religion.

Bowler, Peter J., *Eclipse of Darwinism: Anti-Darwinian Evolution Theories in the Decades around 1900* (Baltimore: Johns Hopkins University Press, 1983), 291 pp.

Emphasis on Lamarck with an extensive bibliography.

Bowler, Peter J., *Evolution: The History of an Idea* (Berkeley: University of California Press, 1984), 412 pp.

Chapters on geology, Lamarck, Darwin, and evolutionary theory's impact on religion, society, and post-Darwinian science.

Clodd, Edward, *Pioneers of Evolution: From Thales to Huxley* (London: Cassell and Company, 1907), 252 pp.

Main chapters on Thales, Lucretius, Augustine, Darwin, Wallace, Spencer, and Huxley.

Eiseley, Loren, *Darwin and the Mysterious Mr. X* (New York: E. P. Dutton, 1979), 278 pp.

Sections on Darwin, Wallace, Lyell, Blyth, and Coleridge.

Eiseley, Loren, *Darwin's Century: Evolution and the Men Who Discovered It* (Garden City: Doubleday Anchor, 1961), 378 pp.

Includes a chapter on minor figures as well as passages concerning Darwin's relations to Malthus, Mendel, and Kelvin.

Gale, Barry G., *Evolution without Evidence: Charles Darwin and the Origin of Species* (Albuquerque: University of New Mexico Press, 1982), 238 pp.

Extensive treatment of Darwin's predecessors and background materials.

Jordanova, L. J., *Lamarck* (Oxford: Oxford University Press, 1984), 118 pp.

Easy introduction to Lamarck.

Millhauer, Milton, *Just Before Darwin* (Middletown: Wesleyan University Press, 1959), 246 pp.

Russett, Cynthia E., *Darwin in America: The Intellectual Response 1865-1912* (San Francisco: W. H. Freeman and Company, 1976), 228 pp.

Vorzimmer, Peter J., *Charles Darwin: The Years of Controversy* (Philadelphia: Temple University Press, 1970), 300 pp.

Considers Darwin's critics during the period 1859-1882.

White, Andrew D., *A History of the Warfare of Science with Theology in Christendom* (New York: D. Appleton and Company, 1898), Volume I, 415 pp., Volume II, 474 pp.

Chapter 1 discusses the Lamarck-Darwin material.

Young, Robert M., *Darwin's Metaphor: Nature's Place in Victorian Culture* (Cambridge: Cambridge University Press, 1985), 341 pp.

Discusses Darwin, Malthus, psychology, and natural theology.

NOTE: Regarding levels of difficulty, nearly all of the primary source materials provide fairly simple reading. Unlike source materials drawn from the physical sciences, no particular proficiency in reading mathematical symbols is required. Though much of this biological material involves a rather tedious compilation of detailed cases, the argumentation can be followed by undergraduates at the introductory level. Regarding secondary source materials, most are written at a relatively accessible level. Finally, with respect to materials suitable for use in various courses, the Philip Appleman, *Darwin: A Norton Critical Edition* is highly recommended. The selections taken from Darwin are carefully chosen, yet sufficiently extensive to provide an excellent presentation of his philosophically significant work. The remaining selections, taken both from Darwin's contemporaries as well as from more recent writers, provide a wide spectrum of positions on a diversity of issues. By judicious selection from these offerings, it should be possible to construct a pattern of readings useful at the introductory level, the advanced undergraduate level or even the graduate level.

Part Three

Curriculum Papers

Workshop on Contemporary Thought

Bowman L. Clarke
Workshop Leader

Workshop Leader's Introduction

Bowman L. Clarke

The Workshop on Contemporary Thought adopted as its task the compilation of an annotated bibliography on certain topics concerned with contemporary natural science, which could be used in planning and offering a course, or courses, concerned with the general topic of the impact of contemporary science on our concept of nature and the concept of God. The topics chosen were not intended to be exhaustive by any means; on the contrary, the number of topics was actually limited by the number of participants in the workshop. From a more comprehensive list, we tried, however, to choose topics about which the present college student has most likely heard and which would, in all likelihood, be of most interest.

The particular topics chosen include: 1) "From Darwin to Psychobiology," which includes material for the consideration of the mind-body problem, of freedom and determinism, and of purpose in nature. 2) "Sociobiology and Recombinant DNA Research," the first part of which raises questions about freedom and determinism and the old nature *versus* nurture question, while the second part raises the serious moral question of the limits of the human dream of controlling nature. 3) "20th Century Physics and its Implications," which is broken down into four sub-topics: relativity theory, quantum mechanics, superstring theory and the anthropic principle, all of which challenge certain theories of nature which have traditionally formed the context in which natural theology has been done and most religious discussions concerned with nature has been carried on. 4) "Feminist Perspectives on Science and Religion," which raises the question of whether or not concepts of nature and of God have been unduly influenced by the fact that males have been dominant in the development of both of them. 5) "Environment, Nature, and God," which brings together our views of nature, our concept of God and certain very critical moral questions in a very timely way. 6) "Futurism," which, in its simplest characterization, is concerned with scientifically predicting possible futures, given the present conditions, and with selecting and influencing the actual future.

These resources are made available to the prospective user in a way in which the user can be selective. This bibliography is not a plan for a course, but incorporates topics and material which might be used in a course, or be selected for several different courses. As an example, a course entitled, "Contemporary Themes in Natural Science and their impact on the concept of God," might be offered embracing the first three topics. In some cases one might wish to construct a course around only one of these topics. The bibliographical material here provided might form a nucleus from which the instructor could work in planning such a course. In the annotations there has been an attempt to evaluate the material of that particular reference in terms of how that material might be useful in the development of a course, or courses.

In cases where need was felt, an introductory section is included, which gives some explanation of the particular topic, its history and reasons why it is included in the present bibliography. "Feminist Perspectives on Science and Religion" and "Futurism" are particularly to be noted in this respect. Under the topic, "20th Century Physics and its Implications," there are included addenda on two of the subtopics, one on Superstring Theory and one on the Anthropic Principle. These two topics are held by many to be on the cutting edge of physics, and it was felt that a more detailed explanation of these ideas would be helpful in this bibliography.

Eighteen

From Darwin to Psychobiology

Stanley Harrison

Books

Ayala, Francisco and Theodosius Dobzhansky, *Studies In The Philosophy of Biology: Reduction and Related Problems*, University of California Press, Los Angeles, CA, 1974, 390 pp.

Nineteen papers plus a transcription of remarks by Jacques Monod devoted to the various problems of reduction in biology. Papers fall into three basic areas: ontological, methodological, and epistemological. Contributors are among top names in biology. Accessible to strong undergraduate students.

Bunge, Mario, *The Mind-Body Problem: A Psychobiological Approach*, Pergamon Press, New York, 1980, 250 pp.

An ambitious attempt to transform the view that man is a set of brain activities into a formalized theoretical framework. Seeks to incorporate latest findings of neurophysiology, psychobiology, and neuropsychology. Wants to retain and defend the need for psychological categories of purpose and thought but avoid any talk of immaterial processes of mind. Some parts would give undergraduates trouble, but a surprising amount of the text is readily accessible.

Gambi, Jeffrey, *Neuroethology: Nerve Cells and the Natural Behavior of Animals*, Sinauer Assoc. Inc., Sunderland, MA, 1984, 415 pp.

An example of recent research into neuronal bases of behavior in specific animals. Special attention to animal signaling. Sections on cockroaches, honeybees, bats, toads, crayfish, cats, and leeches. Packed with information, including many photos, about neuronal organization, feedback behavior, etc. Each of the ten chapters concludes with a summary, questions for thought and discussion, and recommended readings. Quite readable.

Hofer, Myron, *The Roots of Human Behavior: An Introduction To The Psychobiology of Early Development*, W.H. Freeman Co., San Francisco, 1981, 331 pp.

A well organized and well written "text" by a medical man. Contains thorough discussion of neurological foundations of behavior. Separate chapters treat fetal, prenatal and newborn development; great deal of information, with photos and drawings, about neural development and organization, neurobiological maturation in early childhood, with special attention to the way experience influences neural development.

Koestler, Arthur, and J. R. Smythies, *Beyond Reductionism: New Perspectives In The Life Sciences*, Hutchinson and Co., London, 1969.

An oft-cited collection of papers by top names. Many papers devoted to notion of hierarchical structure and its importance for explanations in biology. Still of considerable value.

Lennenberg, Eric H., *Biological Foundations of Language*, John Wiley and Sons, New York, 1967, 489 pp. Includes appendices by Noam Chomsky and Otto Marx.

Frequently referred to as a "classic" of its kind, one that has generated a great deal of literature in response as well as opened up avenues of research. Great attention to neurological aspects of speech and language, stages of language development, language and cognition. A very rich work by a brilliant thinker. Book would be accessible to bright undergraduates.

Monod, Jacques, *Chance and Necessity: An Essay on the Natural Philosophy of Modern Biology*, Alfred A. Knopf, New York, 1971, 199 pp.

A "classic" work by an author who believes that one can explain all features of the natural world in terms of the two principles of chance or randomness and necessity. No need to invoke any form of purpose. The world is an enormous lottery presided over by natural selection. Book has evoked extensive responses.

Schrödinger, Erwin, *What Is Life?*, Macmillan, New York, 1947, 110 pp.

A set of lectures by a renowned physicist who grapples with the theoretical problem of the contrast between the degrees of potential freedom among trillions of molecules in brain and body and the perseverance of essentially invariant patterns of the functioning nervous system. Considers a solution *via* still undiscovered laws of physics to be possible.

Sinnott, Edmund, *Cell and Psyche: The Biology of Purpose*, Univ. of North Carolina Press, Chapel Hill, 1950, 120 pp.

Written by a biologist who sees life as a "mystery." Very readable and useful for opening up basic questions about the forms of biological organization, the orderly control of organic development, and the apparent continuity between the biological and the psychological life of man. Challenges the adequacy of understanding organisms as physico-chemical systems. Sees directiveness as basic to organic life and suggests that the universe as a whole reveals a deeper pattern.

Teyler, Timothy J., *A Primer of Psychobiology*, S. H. Freeman, N.Y., 1984, 181 pp.

An elementary introduction to brain biology and biological bases of behavior. Discusses pain, language, brain aging, etc. Useful for someone just beginning to work on brain biology.

Thorpe, W. H., *Purpose In a World Of Chance*, Oxford Univ. Press, Oxford and New York, 1978, 124 pp.

A biologist's direct response to Monod's *Chance and Necessity*. Argues that science can help clarify the "enduring" reality underlying the transient natural world. Readable and includes useful overview of history of views about "living" matter. Good introduction to importance of genetic code. Focus is on problem of the origin of life and of self-conscious mind. Helpful for locating issues about consciousness and "mind" in nature, including animal communication. Non-technical and well written.

Widroe, Harvey J., M.D. (ed), *Human Behavior and Brain Function*, Charles S. Thomas, Springfield, IL, 1975, 116 pp.

Eight essays on a range of topics such as hemispheric specialization, biological basis of aggressive behavior, effect of drugs, brain subsystems in genesis of schizophrenia, etc. Some use of charts, graphs, and medical schemata.

Wooldridge, Dean E., *The Machinery of The Brain*, McGraw Hill, New York, 1963, 252 pp.

A basic and readable treatment of how the brain works. Emphasis is on a mechanistic model of brain activity.

Articles

Altman, Joseph, "Three Levels of Mentation and The Hierarchic Structure of the Human Brain" in Miller, George A. and Elizabeth Lennenberg, co-editors of *Psychology and Biology of Language and Thought: Essays In Honor of Eric Lennenberg*, Academic Press, New York, 1978.

An essay devoted to the structure and organization of hierarchically related neuropsychic systems. Altman argues that a special system, the anthropocephalon, restricted to the dominant cerebral hemisphere, accounts for the human capacity for language and the symbolic or noetic mentation. Readable and not too technical.

Ayala, Francisco , "Teleological Explanations In Evolutionary Biology," *Philosophy of Science*, 37, 1970, pp. 1-15.

Argues that the ultimate source of explanation in biology is the principle of natural selection which can and should be interpreted as a mechanistic process that can account for the existence in organisms of end-directed structures and processes. While defending teleological explanations as indispensable within biology, he sees no ground for imputing purpose or design to nature considered as a whole, and maintains that this is also Aristotle's view.

Jacobs, Jonathan, "Teleology and Reduction in Biology" in *Biology and Philosophy*, 1, 1986, pp. 389-399.

Argues against reducing biology to the status of a physical science; develops the position that teleology of organisms is intrinsic or basic, that reductionism cannot accommodate this and so cannot explain why lower-level phenomena are as they are. Reductionism is ultimately descriptive and not explanatory because it cannot regard teleological requirements as basic.

Koestler, Arthur, "Free Will In A Hierarchic Context," in *Mind In Nature: Essays On The Interface of Science and Philosophy*, edited by John B. Cobb, Jr., and David Ray Griffin, University Press of America, Washington, D.C., 1977, pp 60-65.

Defends the view that the best way to understand free will is offered by the concept of multi-leveled hierarchic organization; maintains this way as the missing link between panpsychism and Cartesianism.

Mayr, Ernst "Cause and Effect in Biology" in *Towards a Theoretical Biology*, edited by C.H. Waddington, 3 volumes, Aldine Publishing Co., Chicago, IL 1970; Vol. 1, pp. 42-56.

A helpful discussion of basic notions in biology, particularly with respect to how biologists view causality, purpose, and teleology.

Pattee, H. H., "The Problem of Biological Hierarchy" in *Towards a Theoretical Biology, op. cit.*, Vol. 3, pp. 117-136.

A useful discussion of the view that hierarchic organization is the central problem biologists must face for understanding the origin of life, the nature of organic development, biological evolution, and the brain.

Rolston, Holmes, "Life: Religion and the Biological Sciences," in *Science and Religion: A Critical Survey*, by Holmes Rolston, III., Random House, New, York 1987, pp. 81-150.

A provocative challenge to the adequacy of the theory of natural selection when taken alone to account for life, its processes, and the outcomes of evolutionary processes.

Steeped with information drawn from the relevant life sciences. Argues that Darwinian accounts need to be subsumed and recast by a new paradigm which would explain the evident ascent toward complexity and advanced forms of life, an "executive or legislative principle that lures the ascent." The author maintains that bioscience need not block religious belief and that a Christian reinterpretation of nature can integrate suffering, pain, and death as integral to gaining more abundant life.

Ruse, Michael E., "The Revolution in Biology," in *Theoria,* 1, pp. 1-12, 1970.

A discussion of the revolution in biology with reference to Thomas Kuhn's views about what brings on a shift in scientific paradigms. Contains a good treatment of how Darwin's arguments in *The Origin of Species*, when combined with the challenges coming from developments in geology, brought on a serious conceptual revision of the whole natural order.

Weiss, Paul, "The Living System—Determinism Stratified," in *Beyond Reductionism*, edited by Arthur Koestler and J. R. Smythies, The Hutchinson Publishing Co., 1969, pp. 3-42.

Argues that the principle of hierarchic order is revealed in nature as a demonstrable, descriptive fact and that one should view organic entities as open systems or ordered complexes of systems which contain sub-systems; lower levels or sub-systems are part and parcel of a system which is ordered from higher levels.

Weiss, Paul, "Causality: Linear or Systematic," in *Psychology and Biology of Language and Thought, op. cit.* (see Altman above, pp. 13-26, 1978.)

Maintains that attempts to understand brain activity by restricting analysis to individual processes or isolated fragments of what is a living system are misguided. The brain in its wholeness is not reducible to mosaic programs.

Nineteen

Sociobiology and Recombinant DNA Research

Donald A. Crosby

Two New Directions

Two innovative areas in biology that have generated a great deal of discussion in the 1970's and 1980's are Sociobiology and Recombinant DNA research. The first topic raises fundamental questions about human nature, human freedom, the relation of culture to nature, and the scope of scientific theories, especially the theory of evolution. It also provides a new focus for the old nature-nurture debate. The second topic gets into issues of human eugenics, the extent to which humans have the right to alter genetic structures in non-human and human organisms, and how genetic experimentation can be kept safe (or whether it should even be allowed to go on). This second topic also introduces the whole problem of whether the human dream of controlling nature and the future through technology has now reached a crossroads that threatens to unleash forces of destruction lying wholly beyond our control.

Sociobiology

Dawkins, Richard. *The Selfish Gene.* New York: Oxford University Press, 1976.

Dawkins argues that much of animal and human behavior must be understood in terms of the advantages conferred by these behaviors upon the genes of these organisms. He also claims that much of human culture and social organization must be explained in terms of Darwinian evolutionary models of competition and natural selection.

Gregory, Michael S., Anita Silvers, and Diane Sutch (eds.). *Sociobiology and Human Nature: An Interdisciplinary Critique and Defense.* San Francisco, Washington, London: Jossey Bass, 1978.

Outcome of a conference sponsored by NEXA, The Science-Humanities Convergence Program, at San Francisco State University, June, 1977. Various defenses and critiques of sociobiology, with an introduction by E. 0. Wilson and an excellent epilogue by Gregory that summarizes the main issues emerging from the conference papers. Includes papers by Gerald Holton, David Barash, John Searle, Garrett Hardin, Marjorie Grene, Kenneth Boulding, and others.

Hampshire, Stuart. "The Illusion of Sociobiology." *The New York Review of Books,* 25/15 (Oct. 12, 1978).

A clear-headed conceptual analysis and forceful philosophical criticism of assumptions and arguments in sociobiology.

Kitcher, Philip. *Vaulting Ambition: Sociobiology and the Quest for Human Nature.* Cambridge, Massachusetts: The MIT Press, 1985.

This work's principal goal is to explain what sociobiology is, how it relates to evolutionary theory, and "how its ambitious claims rest on shoddy analysis and flimsy argument." This can pave the way for appreciating its contributions to understanding non-human animals while rejecting its premature and untenable speculations about human nature.

Montagu, Ashley (ed.). *Sociobiology Examined.* New York and Oxford: Oxford University Press, 1980.

Contains sixteen chapters critical of sociobiology. Includes two Chapters by Mary Midgley. Other authors include Derek Freeman, S.L. Washburn, Stephen Jay Gould, and Montagu.

Wilson, E. O. *Sociobiology.* Cambridge, Mass.: Harvard University Press, 1975.

Applying natural selection theory to the study of social behavior, Wilson lays the broad theoretical framework, examines the mechanisms of social behavior, and relates these principles to the full range of social species. He concludes with a chapter on the evolution of human social behavior and the adaptive features of organization in human societies.

Wilson, E. O. *On Human Nature.* Toronto, New York, London, Sydney: Bantam Books, 1979.

Explores the thesis that population biology and evolutionary theory can be extended to all forms of social organization, including the human forms. Seeks to draw within its net of scientific materialism such topics as aggression, sex, freedom, morality, and religion.

Recombinant DNA Research

Goodfield, June. *Playing God: Genetic Engineering and the Manipulation of Life*. New York: Random House, 1977.

Examines the science of recombinant DNA to see just what it is and what it can do for good or ill. Focuses on the legal, moral, societal, and ethical issues raised by this science. A well-written discussion for the non-technical reader. Tries to deal fairly with the case for continuing research while also taking seriously the profound problems it poses.

Hanson, Earl D. (ed.). *Recombinant DNA Research and the Human Prospect.* Washington, D.C. : American Chemical Society, 1983.

A sesquicentennial symposium at Wesleyan University, March, 1982. Generally takes an optimistic, enthusiastic view of DNA research and expects responsible behavior from scientists and businesses, in cooperation with broad government guidelines. Much concerned to maintain a positive "public image" of science so that scientists can continue to do their creative work and bestow the benefits of technological innovation on human life.

Lappe, Marc, et al. (eds.). *Ethical and Scientific Issues Posed: Human Uses of Molecular Genetics*. New York: New York Academy of Sciences, 1976.

This series of papers is the result of a conference held on May 15-16, 1975, in New York City. Papers by Daniel Callahan, Gerald Holton, Richard Hull, Robert Neville, and others.

Man and Medicine 2 (Winter 1977).

A special issue with five articles responding to the NIH Guidelines for Recombinant DNA Research of 1976.

Generally critical, the articles raise questions about the adequacy of the guidelines and the circumstances of their promulgation (e.g., an alleged lack of full public participation). Assumptions in the guidelines are identified and critically assessed, and questions about enforcing them are posed. The undertone of the discussions is deep concern about (a) the consequences for science of constraining basic research and (b) the consequences for humans and the ecosystem if such basic research as that into manipulation of genes is not constrained. The NIH guidelines are seen as a small first step in trying to find ways to address these two problems. Open public discussion of the issues is held to be essential before the intellectual and economic investment of DNA research grows greater.

"Recombinant DNA Research." *Bulletin of the Atomic Scientists* 33 (May 1977), 10-33.

In this special section Louis J. Lefkowitz discusses the need for regulatory action; James D. Watson argues that the unsubstantiated dangers are overemphasized; Wallace P. Rowe addresses possible biohazards and appropriate protection of the federal rules; Richard P. Novick indicates that the NIH guidelines must be strengthened, tightened, and made universal; and S. E. Luria focuses on the cost benefit problem and the goals of science. A report by the Cambridge Experimentation Review Board is included.

Rifkin, Jeremy. *Algeny*. New York: Viking Press, 1983.

Sees in the wholesale engineering of life a threat to the existence of life on this planet as serious as nuclear weaponry itself. We are at a crossroads in our technological history that requires a basic critique of "the new technological epoch, the emerging concept of nature that will accompany it, and the intellectual foundation of Western thought that underlies it." We can either "choose to engineer the life of the planet, creating a second nature in our image, or we can choose to participate with the rest of the living kingdom" at the price of giving up our dream of controlling nature and securing our future through technology. The choice is an extremely difficult one, but it is ours. Nontechnical, vigorous, and highly readable.

Twenty

20th Century Physics and its Implications

Ralph Ellis, David Schrader & Stanley Sutphin

The topic of 20TH CENTURY PHYSICS AND ITS IMPLICATIONS is, of course, overwhelming. To fit this into a section of a course in Philosophy of Religion, Philosophy of Science, Philosophy of Nature, Cosmology, Religion and Science, or some other course which is, by its nature, of somewhat broader scope and oriented toward students who may well not have significant background in the discipline of physics requires a careful balance. The major, broad-stroke developments in 20th century physics must initially be laid out both to shake the student out of the Newtonian framework that initially lies implicitly in both his or her thought patterns and language, and to give the background against which the very latest developments in physics can make some sense.

With this in mind, we have divided our proposed "unit" on contemporary physics into four sub-units. The first two sub-units are designed to give that broad-stroke picture. The first sub-unit presents the broad outlines of the theory of relativity: giving the basic idea of relativistic physics; distinguishing, for the student, between the special and the general theories of relativity; and, finally, exposing the student to the non-Euclidean systems of geometry which gain currency as something more than formal games with the acceptance of a relativistic physics. The second sub-unit exposes the student to quantum mechanics: showing in particular how twentieth century physics radically modifies the ontological basis which had been implicit in Newtonian physics and which continues to be implicit in most of our thought patterns and in our language.

The third sub-unit carries the student into one of the latest developments in contemporary physics, Superstring Theory. Superstring Theory is the latest candidate to provide a "Theory of Everything." It proposes at last to unite the understanding of gravitational force that was presented by the theory of relativity with the quantum mechanical understanding of the other three basic forces of contemporary physics (electro-magnetic, and both strong and weak atomic forces). This sub-unit seeks to engage the student with both the problems that have led a number of contemporary physicists to enthusiastically pursue the theory of superstrings and the central challenges that lie ahead in the development of that theory. It also seeks to expose the student to the excitement and life of science at the "cutting edge," where scientific theories have not yet been calcified into dogmas, but are yet tentative projects for human investigators.

The fourth and final sub-unit introduces the student to a recent attempt to draw theological conclusions from our current knowledge of physics. That attempt centers around the anthropic cosmological principle, an up-dated argument from design. The anthropic principle argues from the mind-boggling unlikelihood of the physical universe evolving in a manner capable of producing the world we know to the likelihood of an intelligent designer of that universe. The readings on this last sub-unit present both pro and con views of the anthropic principle.

Suggested Bibliographies

I. RELATIVITY THEORY

Barnett, Lincoln. *The Universe and Dr. Einstein* (New York: Bantam Books, 1948, 1980). 128 pp (available from Aerion House, $4.95)

A good simple explanation, written at a level understandable by the intelligent college student, of the fundamental concepts of relativity physics, using thought experiments as well as actual ones to compel the reader to accept the theory. No math required.

Salmon, Wesley. *Space, Time and Motion* (Minneapolis: University of Minnesota Press, 1980). 160 pp. - $8.95

An especially logical and elegant explanation of special relativity, using algebra and geometry to deduce simply the Lorentz transformation equations from a thought experiment assuming the independence of the velocity of light from the velocity of its source. Also includes clear descriptions of non-Euclidean geometry systems, as well as a concrete description of the Michelson-Morley experiment and experiments confirming Einstein's theory.

Will, Clifford M. *Was Einstein Right? - Putting General Relativity to the Test* (New York: Basic Books, 1986). 272 pp. - $18.95

In contrast to the way most scientific theories come about, Einstein began with a theoretical difficulty, not an experimental problem. Clifford Will has written a book which gives a fascinating and readable account of the modern history of experimental relativity. He writes with a narrative style and recounts the numerous tests which scientists have carried out in the last half-century which verify Einstein's theory. Since this book contains very little mathematics, it will appeal to a broad spectrum of readers from college students to professional physicists. An excellent survey of how general relativity theory has fared experimentally.

Gamow, George. *One, Two, Three, . . . Infinity* (New York: Bantam Books, 1947, 1979). 340 pp.

An excellent, mind-expanding treatment of topology, relativity, the big bang, and paradoxes and mathematical problems involving infinity. Appropriate for intelligent undergraduates.

II. QUANTUM MECHANICS

Davies, P. C. W., and J. R. Brown. *The Ghost in the Atom* (Cambridge: Cambridge University Press, 1986), especially Chapter 1. 156 pp. - $9.95

This book explains clearly and simply some of the most important paradoxes that arise in giving a coherent interpretation of an ontology appropriate for quantum theory, with special attention to the 1982 Alain Aspect experiment that has provoked so much discussion and controversy. The experiment seems to suggest some sort of faster-than-light communication between photons; when one photon in an associated pair is polarized, the other instantaneously becomes polarized in a significant proportion of instances, exceeding Bell's limit. There simply seems to be no currently adequate explanation for the phenomenon. Excellent brief summary of the history of quantum theory as well as contemporary alternative formulations. No math required.

Jauch, J. M. *Are Quanta Real? A Galilean Dialogue* (Bloomington: Indiana University Press, 1973). 106 pp. – $22.50

Though pre-dating the controversial Alain Aspect experiment, this book suggestively explores arguments pro and con about "hidden variable" theories of quantum mechanics. Written in dialogue form, it compares the situation in quantum theory to the period of the Copernican Revolution. Not recommended for students with little or no background in physics.

III. SUPERSTRING THEORY

Green, Michael B. "Superstrings," *Scientific American*, 255:48-60 (September 1986). 13 pp.

Clear, but relatively technical introduction to Superstring Theory, written by one of the two major architects of that theory. Not recommended for students with little or no background in physics.

Schwarz, John H. "Completing Einstein," *Science 85*, 6:60-4 (November 1985). 4 pp.

Excellent introduction to Superstring Theory, written by the other major architect of that theory. Explains clearly, and in a very pleasant and accessible style, what problems Superstring Theory is designed to resolve, what the basic outlines of the theory are, and what lines of research in Superstring Theory may be expected to dominate the work of theorists in the near future.

Michio Kaku and Jennifer Trainer, *Beyond Einstein,* (New York: Bantam, 1987), 288 pp. – $8.95.

Taubes, Gary. "Everything's Now Tied to Strings," *Discover*, 7:34-6 + (November 1986). 12 pp.

Extremely readable, if a bit chatty. Gives the background and development of Superstring Theory. Explains informally the outlines of the theory and the main objections to it. Also gives some good reflections on the sociology of the physics community and of the academic world.

Waldrop, M. Mitchell. "Strings as a Theory of Everything," *Science*, 229:1251-3 (September 20, 1985). 3 pp.

Readable and very good introduction to the development of Superstring Theory. Focusses on the ways in which Superstring Theory emerged as solving important problems arising in particle physics. Somewhat more developmentally oriented than the article by Schwarz. A bit technical in its discussion of dimensionality.

IV. THE ANTHROPIC PRINCIPLE

Barrow, John D. and Frank J. Tipler. *The Anthropic Cosmological Principle* (New York: Oxford University Press, 1986). 706 pp. – $29.95

The foreword is by John A. Wheeler, Center for Theoretical Physics, University of Texas at Austin. One of this book's central themes is creation, whether it concerns the matter content of the universe, the size of the universe, the dimensionality of the universe, or life itself. This is a well-written book, which has been painstakingly researched and includes an immense amount of material on the notion that the universe was not shaped by chance but by a grand design. The authors introduce you to four principle views of the anthropic perspective, each more speculative than the previous one. The book has nearly one hundred pages dealing with the more recent teleological arguments, and even includes a discussion of such process thinkers as Henri Bergson, Samuel Alexander, Alfred North Whitehead, and Charles Hartshorne. However, the book is extremely technical and uses very complex mathematical formulas which will be unintelligible to most people. This book would not be suitable for most courses in philosophy.

Davies, P. C. W. *The Accidental Universe* (New York: Cambridge University Press, 1982). 139 pp. – $11.95

This little book is a systematic attempt to explain the extraordinary, contrived appearance of the physical universe as it has developed in the minds of scientists. Davies is one of the older advocates of the anthropic principle. The book is suitable to anyone who has a general familiarity with basic physics. It should be suitable for students of philosophy and science. Where mathematics is used it almost always involves only elementary algebra.

Davies, P. C. W. *God and the New Physics* (New York: Simon and Schuster, 1983), Chapters 12 and 13. 229 pp.– $7.95

These two chapters are written in a very readable prose style, and are very helpful in setting forth the basic issues of the anthropic principle. Chapter 12, "Accident or Design?" introduces the larger issue of how entropy, or disorder, is closely related to the concepts of probability and arrangement. How do we get low-entropy, or order, out of high-entropy, or disorder? What are the probabilities of this happening by chance? Davies gives three responses to the big bang scenario that produced a remarkably orderly universe. Chapter 13, "Black Holes and Cosmic Chaos," takes up the most perplexing problem of all for physicists, gravity. There is no agreement or understanding among physicists of the thermodynamics of gravitating systems, and concepts such as the entropy of a gravitational field are only vaguely formulated. He concludes this chapter with the statement that "it is hard to resist the impression that the present structure of the universe, apparently so sensitive to minor alterations in the numbers, has been rather carefully thought out." This whole book has a very interesting perspective on how at least some physicists look at many of the problems which we dealt with at the NEH Institute at the University of Georgia. A large portion of the book could be used in a philosophy of religion course or a course on science and religion.

Finkbeiner, Ann. "A Universe in Our Own Image," *Sky and Telescope*, Volume 68, No. (August 1984), pp. 107-11. 4 pp.

This article is written in a popular style and covers rather well the different personalities involved in the anthropic theory from an historical perspective. The author looks at John Wheeler's "participatory" view, which would strike down the classical "observer" theory. Robert Dickey, a physicist at Princeton, was the first to come out with the weak anthropic principle, noting that the laws of nature must be such as to allow, if not force, the formation of carbon, hydrogen, oxygen, and nitrogen, elements necessary for life. The strong view is represented by Barry Collins and Stephen Hawking, who argue that on a large scale the universe appears to be isotropic, the same in all directions, and therefore that the rate of expansion of the universe was very fine-tuned. Finkbeiner's article is good as the quick overview of some of the important developments of the principle.

Gale, George. "Some Metaphysical Perplexities," *International Philosophical Quarterly*, Volume XXVI, No. 4 (December 1986), pp. 393-402. 10 pp.

Gale hypothesizes "that we are entering a phase of scientific activity during which the physicist has out-run his philosophical base camp" and is eager to have philosophy supply some metaphysical support. The author briefly surveys three "tantalizing" philosophical perplexities—the Bootstrap theory, the Anthropic Principle, and quantum-theory. His contention is that all three theories have a methodological and epistemological problem which is consistent with the major crisis of quantum theory: "What is the nature of the scientific object, and how does it interact (if at all) with the scientific observer?" A good article for getting at some of the basic problems of modern physics.

Addendum on Superstring Theory

David E. Schrader

Clearly Einstein's theory of relativity and quantum mechanics constitute the two central theoretical underpinnings of contemporary physics. The central theoretical problem of contemporary particle physics, however, is that these two theoretical underpinnings seem to be incompatible. Einstein's general theory of relativity related the force of gravity to the structure of space and time. It provides an understanding of cosmic-scale phenomena and of the evolution of the universe. Quantum theory, by contrast, provides an understanding of the atomic and subatomic phenomena. Quantum mechanical explanations have been provided for each of the three fundamental forces of nature other than gravitation: the strong and weak atomic forces, and the electromagnetic force. The problem has been that no quantum mechanical explanation of the gravitational force has appeared to be forthcoming.

The theory of superstrings, whether a passing fad or the birth of a new epoch in the history of physics, is the current best shot to provide a "Theory of Everything," a theory which can finally unite all four basic forces of nature. Superstring theory combines the basic idea of string theory, first developed around 1970, with a mathematical structure called supersymmetry.

Early string theories, as well as the current superstring theory, hypothesized that all elementary particles be treated not as dimensionless points, but rather as minuscule one-dimension strings. The current theory of superstrings takes these to have a length of 10^{-33} cm, as much smaller than an atom as an atom is smaller than the solar system. Early string theory was beset with several major problems. First, the quantum mechanical behavior of bosons, the elementary particles such as gauge particles which transmit physical forces, required a space-time structure containing 26 dimensions. Second, the states of lowest energy of the string must be particles travelling faster than the speed of light, which would contradict relativity. Finally, string theories required the existence of a number of massless particles not corresponding to anything yet observed.

Supersymmetry is a mathematical notion which researchers attempted to link with string theory starting in around 1980. In physics, when elements in a set of equations can be interchanged or altered, and still the whole collection displays the same properties, the set is said to have symmetry. Supersymmetry is a symmetry under which the two major classes of subatomic particles, bosons and fermions (quarks, electrons, etc.), can be mathematically interchanged. Supersymmetry, therefore, requires a boson for each fermion and a fermion for each boson. This does lead superstring theories to posit a number of particles which have not yet been observed.

On the positive side, the addition of supersymmetry to string theory does eliminate the faster-than-light particles and reduces the required number of dimensions to 10. The real attraction of superstring theory is that it makes it possible to consider all four fundamental forces as various aspects of a common underlying principle. Perhaps equally important, the unification of forces is accomplished in a way determined almost uniquely by the requirement of logical consistency. One of the most appealing results here is that gravity, the hitherto recalcitrant force, is not merely accommodated, it is in fact also required by the demand that the theory be internally consistent.

There are two crucial issues related to the understanding of superstring theory that I think need to be mentioned here. The first involves the 10 dimensions required by the theory. Superstring theory supposes that at the time of the original "big bang," there were 10 dimensions, all of them compacted into a virtual point. From the time of the bang, four dimensions, one temporal and three spatial, expanded, while the other six remained compacted. One might think of this along the line of a common garden hose, which at appropriate distance will appear one-dimensional. Similarly, at the original "bang," all of the forces were also united. With the earliest stages of expansion (we may speak here in terms of seconds), symmetries started to break down, resulting in the separating of the force into the four forces with which we are now familiar.

The second issue involves the new particles required by supersymmetry. This is an issue involving some considerable ambiguity. On the one hand, the prediction of these new particles does offer the chief hope in principle for testing superstring theory. Yet the flip side of this is that the investigation of such extremely small particles requires machinery employing enormous amounts of energy, presumably energy far beyond what will be available to us in the foreseeable future.

Superstring theory raises a collection of intriguing philosophical issues. At the present point, superstring theory is substantially just a mathematical formulation. Physicists have no particular idea of the basic principles on which the theory is based. Why, for example, should the string structure be so successful in leading to a unification of the four forces? What is the importance of the mathematics working out right in physical theory? Can mathematical elegance carry theory as far as superstrings with very little in the way of experimental confirmation? While superstring theory is yet too new for either philosophers or physicists to have made much in the way of metaphysical speculation based on it, if the theory does continue to gain currency among physicists, such speculation is surely inevitable. At this point, it is interesting to compare the role of mathematics in superstring theory with the role of mathematics in Plato's *Timaeus*. It appears that things may not have changed all that much. Whether this is good or bad, and why it is either good or bad, are themselves fundamentally interesting questions.

Addendum on the Anthropic Principle

Stanley T. Sutphin

The anthropic principle has roots in an observation by P.A.M. Dirac, a theoretical physicist at Cambridge University who won the 1933 Nobel Prize for physics. In 1937, he noticed a striking coincidence between certain cosmological numbers. One such number is the mass of the visible universe measured in terms of the mass of a proton. The mass of the universe, or the number of charged particles, is roughly 10^{80}. The second number is the age of the universe in the units of time it takes light to travel across what the physicist calls the classical electron radius (about 10^{-23} seconds), approximately 10^{40}. The third value is the constant that measures the strength of gravity in terms of the electrical force between two protons. Gravity is about 10^{40} times weaker. Dirac felt that it was remarkable that the number 10^{40} (or its double) kept appearing in cosmology and atomic physics. He asserted that such a coincidence was due to some deep connection in nature between cosmology and atomic theory. Dirac pointed out that there was a problem with this connection. The first number, the mass of the universe, and the third value, the gravitational coupling constant, are believed not to change. If the coincidences did point to some fundamental law in nature, then all three quantities would have to change together or not at all. He suggested that the gravitational constant and the mass of the universe must change with time. Dirac never uncovered any deeper law of nature that solved the problem, but the large number hypothesis continued to fascinate physicists.

In 1961, Robert Dickey, a physicist at Princeton University, published a short paper in which he disagreed with Dirac. Dickey argued that the mass of the universe and the gravitational constant do not change. These two numbers are linked, he said, by Mach's Principle, which states that an object's inertia is due to some influence exerted by all the other matter in the universe. Thus, if the mass of the universe stays the same, the forces of inertia and gravity must do likewise. Dickey pointed out that if these two numbers do not vary, even though the age of the universe does, and if all three are momentarily in peculiar correspondence, then we must live at a very special time. Dickey believed that he could see the reason for this possibility. Elements such as carbon, nitrogen, and oxygen are prerequisites for life as we know it. But these elements did not exist in large quantities in the hydrogen-rich primeval universe. Sufficient time had to elapse for succeeding generations of stars to generate larger proportions of these heavy elements, which are believed to be the results of the nucleo-synthesis which occurs inside stars. During the big bang, temperatures high enough to synthesize heavy elements were available, but only for a duration of a few minutes. Only the element helium (irrelevant for life) was produced in abundance. On the other hand, in stellar interiors, extremely high temperatures are available for billions of years, enabling a large fraction of the stellar material to become converted into heavy elements. In order for these elements to become the chemical building blocks of life, they must be dispersed around the galaxy. This can occur when a star reaches the end of its life, and has exhausted its nuclear fuel. If the star is rather massive, then it is likely to explode violently as a supernova, spewing its contents into interstellar space. Life cannot form in the universe, Dickey reasoned, until at least one generation of stars has passed through this life cycle, and seeded the galaxy with the supernova debris containing carbon. On the other hand, the consumption of hydrogen fuel by stars is irreversible, so that this cycle cannot be repeated *ad infinitum*. After a few generations of stars, the galaxy's supply of nuclear fuel will become severely depleted, and new stars (at least stable stars like the sun) will become rather rare. The galaxy will then begin to cool, and one imagines life will become impossible.

Thus Dickey concluded that, contrary to our original supposition, the age of the universe is not a "random choice" from a wide range of possible choices, but is limited by the criteria for the existence of human beings. Cosmologists have calculated that the present age of the universe is roughly what Dickey reasoned it must be, which means that if the universe were much younger or much older, we would not be here. Dickey's statement was the earliest formulation of the WEAK anthropic principle; however, he did not use this term for it.

The anthropic principle was submerged in the scientific community for the next decade but resurfaced again in 1973, at an International Astronomical Union symposium at which Brandon Carter, an astrophysicist from Cambridge University, presented what has come to be known as the STRONG anthropic principle.

Carter argued that nature has evidently picked the values of the fundamental constants in such a way that typical stars lie very close to the boundary of convection instability. If gravity were *very* slightly weaker, or electromagnetism *very* slightly stronger (or the electron slightly less massive relative to the proton), all stars would be red dwarfs. A correspondingly tiny change the other way, and they would all be blue giants. Carter argued that a star's surface convection plays an important role in planetary formulation, so that a world where gravity was very slightly less weak might have no planets. In either case, weaker or stronger, the universe would be radically different.

In the same year, two other Cambridge physicists, Barry Collins and Stephen Hawking, pointed out still another anthropic coincidence. They noted that not only is the strength of gravity critical to life, but so is the rate at which the universe expands. They addressed the question: "Why is the universe isotropic (i.e., as we look outward from Earth, the universe presents the same aspect on the large scale in whichever direction we look – uniform in every direction)?" They argued that an anisotropic universe might produce vast quantities of heat, which would prevent the formation of galaxies by exerting strong radiation pressure. Obviously such circumstances would not favor life as we know it. They reasoned that, in general, the universe ought to become more and more anisotropic as it expands. However, if the expansion rate is exactly matched to the gravitating power, then it will remain isotropic. In order for large-scale isotropy to coexist with small-scale inhomogeneity, or gravitational clumping, the rate of expansion must be precisely tuned. If the cosmos had expanded too quickly, with only a slight deviation from its actual rate, galaxies could not have held together – matter would not have been able to reach the "escape velocity" needed to overcome its mutual gravitational attraction. Collins and Hawking answered their question, "Why is the universe isotropic?" with "Because we exist." This answer has bothered some physicists who consider it tautological.

The answer to this question brings us to the third anthropic view, that of the MANY-WORLDS. Carter, Collins, and Hawking all assert the possibility that there are a large number of universes, with all possible combinations of initial data and values of fundamental constants. The first person to propose the many worlds view was Hugh Everett, a student of Wheeler's. In 1957 he wrote in his doctoral dissertation that the observer is not external to the object observed. Both are members of the same ensemble. Everett takes the observer-object system, starting with the paradoxical single electron, along with all the others possible, and includes it in a universal wave function. In his theory all possible quantum worlds are actually realized, and coexist in parallel with each other. Thus, every time an electron faces two choices, both alternatives occur, and the entire universe divides into two. Each universe is complete with inhabitants (whose brains and minds have apparently been bifurcated), each set of which believes that the electron has abruptly opted for one of the alternatives. The innumerable new universes branch off from ours at every moment to fulfill all the possibilities open to each elementary particle. We are aware of following only ONE such universe, corresponding to one track of possibilities and we can not travel from one to the other in ordinary space and time. As bizarre as this view seems, some theorists have pointed out that Everett's interpretation is just as compatible with experiment as the COPENHAGEN view. Brandon Carter has applied this MANY-WORLD view to the Big Bang and envisaged it resulting in the "world ensemble." In one universe, the strength of gravity might be such that all stars are blue giants, in another all red dwarfs. Only very select universes have the right conditions for life. All the others go unnoticed.

The fourth theory is that proposed by John A. Wheeler and is, perhaps, the most extreme. One implication of the Copenhagen interpretation is that the observer affects reality by the act of measurement. Wheeler has written that "Participator is the incontrovertible new concept given by quantum mechanics." Therefore, he cannot picture a universe built on elementary quantum phenomena which does not contain observers, or what he insists are "participators." If all particles and forces are built of billions upon billions of these elementary quantum phenomena, then to get the world going, you have to have the acts of the observer-participant. That participant need not be conscious or alive, because it is anything that completes an elementary quantum phenomenon.

Twenty-one

Feminist Perspectives on Science and Religion

Robert C. Smith & John Hammond

These materials can provide the basis for a course on this two-fold topic, or selections could be used to make up parts of courses in philosophy of science and philosophy of religion.

The following are some common themes which could be used to help integrate the study of feminist commentary on science and religion:

1. Feminists claim that male bias has deeply influenced the institutional forms and practice of both science and religion.

2. As a result, both science and religion express, and serve to perpetuate, forms of male domination in society.

3. Exclusion of women and of women's viewpoint has led to one-sidedness and distortion in both of these human institutions.

4. Both science and religion would benefit from the inclusion of women's unique experience, values, and ways of understanding.

5. Some feminists claim that "sexist" images of nature have played a role in supporting patterns of male bias in science and religion.

These authors are led to critically examine Western views of nature as part of their program of reforming science and religion.

Feminist Perspectives on Science

During the liberation movements of the 1960's, women became increasingly aware of their historical status as disadvantaged. The exclusion of women from science was, of course, only one aspect of this condition. Women were under-represented in science, and those who did make it into the profession were often denied equal access to resources and advancement. Affirmative action at various levels made slow progress in dealing with this workplace situation. But perhaps more important, many women began to have misgivings about the institution of science itself, its methods and implicit values. The discussion of this matter by feminist critics over the last decade has brought to view the following contentions:

1. The popular image of science as the disinterested pursuit of knowledge guided only by logical and rational constraints is at best an oversimplification. Science is rather a "social institution" whose development reflects the impress of certain dominant historical social values, most notably those of a patriarchal social order.

2. Male ("androcentric") bias has deeply informed science: its methods, the understanding of the aims of research, and the understanding among scientists of the qualities that make a good scientist. Some women authors have explored a further level of historical and psychological analysis, claiming that a peculiar image of nature underlies and supports this traditional conception of western science. This is the idea of nature as feminine, passive, as harboring secrets which must be teased or forced from "her," etc. (Cf. Bacon's Star Chamber!)

3. Along with the above "deconstructive" critiques, there has recently emerged a positive "reconstructive" discussion, aimed at tracing a new vision of what science could be like if freed from male biases. There is some consensus here that women's experience and skills are different from men's and that science could profit from this additional human resource. As one writer puts it, "Gender matters not simply because of the occupational and educational rights of one half of the population, but also because of what that half can bring to the total of human knowledge."

Two further points: (1) Feminists generally have criticized the theory that gender differences are biologically determined. Feminist critics of science typically recur to this theme in making their case for ideological bias in science. Thus biology has come under a lot of fire on this issue. (2) The claim that science is gender-biased has been aimed mainly at biology and the social sciences. But some authors argue that the physical sciences (often viewed as models of objectivity), and even mathematics, reflect certain male values and biases.

BIBLIOGRAPHY

Bleier, Ruth, *Science and Gender: A Critique of Biology and Its Theories on Women*. New York: Pergamon Press, 1984.

An analysis of the role of science in helping to legitimate the differences in the social and economic positions of women. The author attempts to show how scientists reinforce the inferior roles of women by arguing that gender differences are biologically determined and thus "nature." The main critical discussion is directed at sociobiological theory and methods, attempts to base sex differences in the anatomy of the brain, and "man-the-hunter" theories of human origins.

Bleier concludes that women's position reflects "patriarchal social orders" which have defined both the "private and public worlds" of human beings. She also argues that the inclusion of women's unique experience and thought modes can help to create a more humane science. Frequently references, and serves as introduction to much current literature. Non-technical, readable, suitable for all college levels.

Harding, Jan, *Perspectives on Gender and Science.* New York: The Falmer Press, 1986.

An anthology of essays by current feminist authors. The approach is mainly sociological and psychological. Topics include: studies of the experience of women in science, factors that discourage women in the field, identification of masculine qualities in science, theories of the origin of gender identity, qualities in science, theories of the origin of gender identity, and the advantages for science of greater inclusion of women. For all college levels, good general reference.

Harding, Sandra, *The Science Question in Feminism.* Ithaca: Cornell University Press, 1986.

The author examines recent trends in feminist critiques of science. The book is liberally referenced and the reader is introduced to the views of many current authors. There is an extensive, up-to-date bibliography and an index. Mainly emphasizes biology and the social sciences, but there is a provocative section on male bias in the physical sciences and mathematics.

This is the most comprehensive of the books listed, and the most demanding of the reader. It is directed toward readers with some familiarity with philosophical methods and terms.

Harding, Sandra, and Hintikka, Merrill B., *Discovering Reality: Feminist Perspectives on Epistemology, Metaphysics, Methodology, and Philosophy of Science*. Boston: Reidel, 1983.

A collection of interdisciplinary essays with two focuses. The authors claim to disclose that traditional epistemological and metaphysical assumptions mirror and support patriarchal belief and practice, thus distorting models of knowledge and scientific inquiry toward an emphasis on abstraction from the physical, concrete world and on hierarchical dualism, e.g. mind-body. A second goal is to argue that women's experience differs (from men's) because their (women's) emphasis is on opposition to dualisms, on concreteness and continuity. These distinctive aspects, it is claimed, either can form the basis for a feminist perspective on epistemology, metaphysics, methodology, and the philosophy of science, or can be combined with male experience for a fully human understanding of the issues.

Suitable primarily for graduate collections, but usable by advanced undergraduates.

Keller, Evelyn Fox, *Reflections on Gender and Science*. New Haven: Yale University Press, 1985.

A principal aim of the author is "the reclamation of science as a human instead of a masculine project, and the renunciation of the division of intellectual and emotional labor that maintains science as a male preserve." The book falls into three parts, as the author considers "the network of gender associations in science" first historically, then psychoanalytically, and finally scientifically and philosophically.

Keller claims that the image of science and scientific work has been guided by a view of nature as female. This underlies, she contends, "the deeply rooted mythology that casts objectivity, reason, and mind as male, and subjectivity, feeling, and nature as female."

The writing is non-technical, readable, suitable for undergraduate on up.

Watts, Alan, *Nature, Man, and Woman*. New York: Pantheon, 1958.

This book anticipates some of the "deep" themes in feminist critiques of science. Watts argues that there are parallels between Western men's attitudes toward women and toward nature. In both cases, attitudes of domination, exploitation, and control have been paramount. He suggests that this orientation is reflected in Western science, and he speculates on the character of an alternative approach to studying nature. Watts takes inspiration from Eastern views of nature.

Feminist Perspectives on Religion

"There is something wonderful happening. One could call it a reclamation of something lost or forgotten, certainly something distorted or suppressed. It comes by many names. It is half of divine consciousness omitted in traditional worship of the Father God. SHE is reemerging today as the result of the inner work of a growing number of women artists who while in search of themselves amid confusion of masculine and feminine roles in their own time came upon a larger vision for all time—a mystical feminine revelation." Louise Calio has written the above statement in *The Rebirth of the Goddess*. The statement could be multiplied dozens of times over.

The women's movement has challenged feminists to look anew at the role of the feminine principle in history, society, and religious thought. It has given them the courage to think for themselves, to write their own texts, and create their own mythology. Further it has led to the development of a feminist theology taking many diverse forms based on ancient goddess models and again on reconstructions of a deity androgynous in nature pushing out exclusively masculine features and incorporating the neglected aspects of deity. Some have called this perspective the*a*logy (a term coined by Naomi Goldenberg in *Changing of the Gods*). This *thealogy* has ripened into a powerful thought expression that finds expression in many scholarly disciplines, creative arts, and woman-centered political activities.

Feminist spirituality had its origin less than twenty years ago in scholarly research. Profound questions about the origins of male domination arose: if female authority was honored in some contemporary "primitive" societies, what was the world like thousands of years ago when we were all hunter-gatherers? These scholars have raised a host of questions about the origin of patriarchy: How and why did it come about? In what ways can it and must it be reversed in egalitarian society? This questioning became part of the social criticism of the past two decades when political activists challenged many traditional assumptions about societal roles, including the relationships between men and women, women and religion, women and nature, and religion and society.

Many feminists choose to remain within the Church because they find Christ's teachings are powerful enough to withstand any subsequent sexist theology. They are exploring traditional Christian and Biblical themes from a woman-centered perspective, seeking a god who need not be rejected in the pursuit of true liberation for all. Christian feminists yearn to see a reflection of the Divine in themselves just as much as women who have utterly rejected patriarchal religious institutions. Both those committed to finding new meaning within existing religious institutions and those outside them are interested in new ways of looking at old religions, in works that create new myths, and in new patterns of social and spiritual interaction. Rosemary Ruether, a leading feminist constructive theologian, has written: "The uniqueness of feminist theology lies not in its use of the criterion of experience but in its use of women's experience, which has been almost entirely shut out of theological reflection in the past . . . theologically speaking, whatever diminishes or denies the full humanity of women must be presumed not to reflect the divine or an authentic nature of things, or to be the message of an authentic redeemer or a community of redemption."

1. General readings

For those unfamiliar with the dynamism of the feminist critique of nature and the concept of the divine, recent essays by representative feminists is a good place to begin.

Christ, Carol P. and Plaskow, Judith, eds. *Womanspirit Rising: A Feminist Reader in Religion*, New York: Harper and Row, 1979. 287 p.

A collection of essays on woman's place in traditional and post-patriarchal religion that is an excellent starting place for the new reader. The first group of articles lays bare the sexism of Western religion; the second section deals with the history of women in the religious of the Near East and Europe; the third is concerned with attempts to refeminize Christianity and Judaism; and the final section describes the new paths in forging spiritual thought.

Spretnak, Charlene, ed. *The Politics of Women's Spirituality: Essays on the Rise of Spiritual power within the Feminist Movement*. Garden City: Anchor Books, 1982. 590 p.

This is one of the most important books to have arisen from the women's spirituality movement. In addition to the better known feminist authors, feminist spirituality is discussed by Black, Asian, and Native American women. Contains an extensive bibliography on women's spirituality, especially in its political context.

2. Reconstruing Nature

Feminist rethinking on the issue of the pyramid of dominance, status, and the anthropocentric illusion.

Gray, Elizabeth Dodson, *Green Paradise Lost*, Wellesley, MA: Roundtable Press, 1981. 166 p.

An exploration of the mythic and psycho-sexual roots of our Western imaging of nature. Part I is about our "fall" into the illusion of human domination. Part II explores what happens when domination and mastery are no longer the major inner drives shaping what we seek to do in the world. This "re-mything of Genesis" involves a new vision of reality and gives us a new sense of human identity. Professor Gray is coordinator of the Theological Opportunities Program at Harvard Divinity School and is an environmentalist and futurist.

3. Feminist Interpretations of Biblical Notions of God

Some feminists contend that traditional ideas of God are unbiblical in that they exclusively focus on patriarchal idea of God to reinforce their male bias and that Scripture contains a host of feminine conceptions of the divine.

Mollenkott, Virginia Ramey. *The Divine Feminine: the Biblical Imagery of God as Female*. New York: Crossroad, 1983. 120 p.

This theologian writes that if the good news of Christianity is to reach all people, than theological language must be used by which women as well as men can identify with God. Many feminine images of the Godhead can be found in both Testaments, such as Jesus comparing himself to a mother hen protecting her chickens, or to the woman who searches for a lost coin. There are also images of God as earth, wind, fire, and water, as a woman in labor, and as Lady Wisdom.

4. Reconstruing the divine

The issues here are many: patriarchal interpretations and ideas of divine essence and Aristotelian notions of determinacy that generally have gone hand in hand and been used to justify the idea that God has consigned nature to man's dominion as that which should be ruled over. Feminists reverberate to the idea that we should enter into relation with nature and appreciate indeterminacy. They have applauded Capra's *Tao of Physics* model which suggests that everything in the universe flows together.

Ruether, Rosemary Radford, *Sexism and God-Talk: Toward a Feminist Theology*. Boston: Beacon Press, 1983. 289 p.

A working paradigm for a feminist theology emerges from Ruether's wide-ranging study. Grounding her analysis in women's experience, she addresses the major themes of Christian theology—images of the divine; nature and creation; the anthropology of sex differences; Christology: Mariology; the consciousness of evil; and eschatology. This work connects woman-body-nature and makes a major contribution toward an emergent theology.

Oddie, William. *What Will Happen to God*? London: SPCK, 1984. 159 p.

A Christian theologian attempts to evaluate and refute the feminist critique of God-talk. He views the feminist hermeneutics with suspicion, as the first of a series of dominos. Once it has fallen, others will follow—so the argument goes. Oddie's argument is lucid, but of the same genre that opposed John Robinson's *Honest to God* over two decades ago.

5. Rebirth of the Goddess Models

Goldenberg, Naomi. *Changing of the Gods: Feminism and the End of Traditional Religions*. Boston: Beacon Press, 1979, 152 p.

Goldenberg writes of the challenge feminism represents to patriarchal religion and of the new visions women are creating of a wide range of images of spirituality, including "return to the goddess" and a host of other spiritual practices now in vogue, such as witchcraft. She sees feminist theology being utilized as a new kind of psychology based in part on Jungian principles and on a respect for myth and symbol.

Carson, Anne. *Feminist Spirituality and the Feminine Divine: An Annotated Bibliography*. Trumansburg, NY: Crossing Press, 1986.

A 739-entry annotated bibliography whose focus tilts toward the occult and esoteric rather than the theological. This volume is a delight to discover and should provide social scientists of religious and quasi-religious phenomena source material to study for some time.

6. Other bibliographies

Loeb, Catherine, *Women's Studies: A Recommended Core Bibliography* 1980-1985. Littleton, Colorado: Libraries Unlimited, 1987.

Steinman, Esther, *Women's Studies: A Recommended Core Bibliography*. Littleton, Colorado: Libraries Unlimited, 1979.

From earliest times to 1979. Continued by Loeb (above).

Twenty-two

Environment, Nature, and God

Jack Weir & Holmes Rolston, III

Attfield, Robin, *The Ethics of Environmental Concern*. New York: Columbia University Press, 1983.

Barbour, Ian G., ed., *Earth Might Be Fair: Reflections on Ethics, Religion, and Ecology*. Englewood Cliffs, NJ: Prentice-Hall, 1972.

Essays were written out of continuing annual conversations between the contributors. Articles include: Frederick Ferré, "Explanation in Science and Theology"; John J. Compton, "Science and God's Action in Nature"; Daniel Day Williams, "Changing Concepts of Nature"; Huston Smith, "Tao Now: An Ecological Testament"; William G. Pollard, "The Uniqueness of the Earth"; Harold K. Schilling, "The Whole Earth Is the Lord's: Toward a Holistic Ethic"; Roger L. Shinn, "Science and Ethical Decision: Some New Issues"; Ian G. Barbour, "Attitudes Toward Nature and Technology."

Barbour, Ian G., *Technology, Environment, and Human Values*. New York: Praeger, 1980. 331 pp. Index.

Thorough treatment from a religious and "resource" perspective. Chapters include: Attitudes Toward Nature; Attitudes Toward Technology; Human Values; Environmental Values; Political Processes; Pollution and

Land Use; Costs, Benefits, and Risks; Assessment Methods; Energy Options; Food and Population; Resources and Growth; New Directions. Barbour explains and assesses numerous and varied sources. Both individuals and sociopolitical institutions are addressed. In the final chapter, Barbour calls for what he considers to be "significant departures" from the status quo, such as environmental criteria instead of economic ones, shifting to labor intensive technologies, and either vegetarianism or a severely reduced meat diet. Readable for undergraduates.

Barbour, Ian G., *Western Man and Environmental Ethics*. Menlo Park, CA: Addison-Wesley, 1973.

Birch, Charles, and John B. Cobb, Jr., *The Liberation of Life: From the Cell to the Community*. Cambridge: Cambridge University Press, 1981.

Blackstone, William T., ed., *Philosophy and Environmental Crisis*. Athens: University of Georgia Press, 1974. 140 pp. No index.

Eight important early articles that, despite their datedness, emphasize the basic problems and options. Articles include: Eugene P. Odum, "Environmental Ethic and the Attitude Revolution"; William T. Blackstone, "Ethics and Ecology"; Joel Feinberg, "The Rights of Animals and Unborn Generations"; Charles Hartshorne, "The Environmental Results of Technology"; Walter H. O'Briant, "Man, Nature and the History of Philosophy"; Nicholas Rescher, "The Environmental Crisis and the Quality of Life"; Robert G. Burton, "A Philosopher Looks at the Population Bomb"; and Pete A. Y. Gunter, "The Big Thicket: A Case Study in Attitudes Toward Environment."

Brennan, Andrew, *Thinking About Nature: An Investigation of Nature, Value, and Ecology*. London: Routledge, and Athens, Georgia: University of Georgia Press, 1988. 235 + xiii pages. Bibliography. Index.

Callicott, J. Baird, *In Defense of the Land Ethic: Essays in Environmental Philosophy*. Albany: State University of New York Press, 1989. 224 pages. Index.

Callicott, J. Baird, and Roger Ames, *Environmental Philosophy: The Nature of Nature in Asian Traditions of Thought*. Albany: State University of New York Press, 1989.

Carmody, John, *Ecology and Religion: Toward a Christian Theology of Nature*. New York: Paulist Press, 1983. 185 pp. Annotated bibliography. No index.

Aimed at undergraduates, this book is a religious treatment from the perspective of Roman Catholicism. Carmody calls for a new Christian theology of nature and adapts Bernard Lonergan's theology to this end. Part I surveys the current issues in ecology (as they relate to religion), and Part II presents a theology of nature drawn from biblical, theological, and ethical sources.

Carson, Rachel. *Silent Spring*. New York: Fawcett Crest/ Ballentine Books, 304 pp., Index. 1962. Paper.

A classic. Presents vivid and emotive depictions of environmental abuses, particularly from chemical and toxic substances. Unless humans change present trends, there will be a "silent spring."

Clark, Stephen R. L., *The Moral Status of Animals*. Oxford: Oxford University Press, 1977, 1984. 221 pp. Index. Works cited. Paper.

Aristotelian approach to animals, i.e., animals ought to have lives according to their kind. Vegetarianism is endorsed. Includes poetry and emotive materials. Readable but wordy.

Cobb, John B., Jr., *Is It too Late? A Theology of Ecology*. Beverley Hills, CA: Bruce, 1972.

Sketches a view of nature based on process theology.

Devall, Bill, and George Sessions, *Deep Ecology*. Salt Lake City: Gibbs M.Smith, 1985. 267 pp. Appendixes. Bibliography. List of action groups. Paper.

Arguing that "shallow" approaches are not going to resolve the current crisis, "deep ecology" has been proposed by the Norwegian philosopher and environmental activist Arne Naess (founder and former editor of *Inquiry*). "Deep ecology" is a nonanthropocentric movement calling for the overthrow of the current social, political, and value system in favor of biospheric egalitarianism. In practical actions, generally high-energy (symbolized by electricity), high-technology (symbolized by steel), and political centralization (symbolized by the industrial nation-states) are rejected in favor of low-energy, low-technology, and small, decentralized communities. This book is easy reading and is somewhat of a handbook of the movement. It explains and criticizes various viewpoints, and presents suggestions for resistance.

Dubos, René, *The Wooing of the Earth*. New York: Charles Scribner, 1980.

Durrell, Lee, *State of the Ark*. New York: Doubleday/Gaia Books, 1986.

A large format, slick-paper book with numerous pictures and diagrams. Generally assesses the current plight of the planet. The "Gaia" theme, namely, that the holistic biosphere is alive, is minor.

Elliot, Robert, and Arran Gare, eds., *Environmental Philosophy*. State College: Pennsylvania State University Press, 1983.

Elsdon, Ron, *Bent World: A Christian Response to the Environmental Crisis*. Downers Grove, Illinois: InterVarsity Press, 1981.

Environmental Ethics, vols. 1- ,(1979-). Edited by Eugene C. Hargrove at the University of Georgia.

The premier journal in the field. The editorial policy is to be an interdisciplinary journal in applied ethics and to maintain a clear focus on ecology or environment in all the articles. However, most of the articles are by philosophers, not scientists. Book reviews are included.

Graber, Linda H., *Wilderness as Sacred Space*. Washington, D.C.: American Association of Geographers, 1976.

Gray, Elizabeth Dodson, *Green Paradise Lost*. Wellesley, Massachusetts: Roundtable Press, 1981. (Earlier published as *Why the Green Nigger?*).

Hargrove, Eugene C., ed., *Beyond Spaceship Earth: Environmental Ethics and the Solar System*. San Francisco: Sierra Club Books, 1986. 336 pages. Bibliographical Note. Index. Paper.

Hargrove, Eugene C., *Foundations of Environmental Ethics*. Englewood Cliffs: Prentice-Hall, Co., 1989. 240 pages. Index. Paper.

Hargrove, Eugene C., ed., *Religion and Environmental Crisis*. Athens: University of Georgia Press, 1986. 222 pp. Bibliography. Paper.

Eleven articles with an introduction by Frederick Ferré. The focus is broadly religious, encompassing Eastern and Western, ancient and modern religions. Articles are on the environmental issue as it relates to: Greek polytheism (J. Donald Hughes); American Indian religion (Gerard Reed); Judaism (Jonathan Helfand); the Old Testament (Susan Power Bratton); biblical accounts of nonhuman organisms (Martin LaBar); Taoism (Po-keung Ip); Islam (Iqtidar H. Zaidi); Catholicism (including Latin America) (Sophie Jakowski); the Christian realism of Reinhold Niebuhr (Robert H. Ayers); and process theology (John B. Cobb, Jr. and Jay McDaniel). The articles are brief and readable

Hart, John, *The Spirit of the Earth: A Theology of the Land*. New York: Paulist Press, 1984.

Joranson, Philip N., and Ken Butigan, eds., *Cry of the Environment: Rebuilding the Christian Creation Tradition*. Santa Fe, New Mexico: Bear, 1984.

Kohák, Erazim, *The Embers and the Stars*. Chicago: University of Chicago Press, 1984. 269 pp. Bibliography. Index.

Lappé, Frances Moore, *Diet for a Small Planet.* 10th ed. New York: Bantam Books, 1982. 496 pp. Index. Paper.

The main contribution of this book is its exposure of multinational corporate control of agriculture and of the commercial food industry. For capitalistic profit, underdeveloped nations and vast wilderness areas are being polluted, exploited, and destroyed. Although Lappé's proposal for solving the food crisis and poverty—by boycotting meat—is too simplistic and is empirically questionable as to its effectiveness, her treatment is stimulating, provocative, and easily read. Includes recipes and nutritional information.

Leopold, Aldo, *A Sand County Almanac.* New York: Ballentine Books, 1966. Paper.

A classic. Originally published in 1949 by Oxford University Press. The founder of ecological ethics, Leopold was an environmentalist and forester at the University of Wisconsin. The book is homespun reflections on the author's experiences and travels. The book would serve as an inspirational introduction to environmental ethics and to the "holistic" approach. Easy reading.

Linzey, Andrew, *Animal Rights: A Christian Assessment of Man's Treatment of Animals.* London: SCM Press, 1976.

Midgley, Mary, *Animals and Why They Matter.* Athens: University of Georgia Press, 1983. 158 pp. Index. Paper.

Naess, Arne, *Ecology, Community, and Lifestyle.* New York: Cambridge University Press, 1988.

Nash, Roderick, *Wilderness and the American Mind.* 3rd rev. ed. New Haven: Yale University Press, 1982.

A review of various understandings of ecological diversity and wilderness. Includes chapters on the philosophy of wilderness and the official "wilderness" policy. Has chapters on Muir, Thoreau, and Leopold.

Norton, Bryan G., ed., *Preservation of Species.* Princeton: Princeton University Press, 1986.

Norton, Bryan G., *Why Preserve Natural Variety?* Princeton: Princeton University Press., 1987.

Passmore, John, *Man's Responsibility for Nature.* New York: Charles Scribner's Sons, 1974. 213 pp. Index.

An influential early treatment, Passmore's book is easy reading. Part I is a brief historical survey of Western attitudes and approaches to nature and the environment. Part II is now dated and treats four problems: pollution, conservation, preservation, and population. Finally, Part III is Passmore's conclusions. He takes an anthropocentric and resource (utilitarian) approach.

Regan, Tom, *The Case for Animal Rights.* Berkeley: University of California, 1983. 425 pp. Bibliography. Index. Paper.

Probably the most thorough treatment of the issues raised by human relationships to animals. Regan tries to modify Kant to include mammalian animals, which he argues have "inherent" value that prohibits using them as mere means to ends. Excellent analyses and criticisms of the leading positions. Readable, although some parts might be difficult for undergraduates.

Regan, Tom, ed., *Earthbound: New Introductory Essays in Environmental Ethics.* New York: Random House, 1984. 371 pp. Index. Paper.

The ten articles in this anthology were written specifically for this volume. Except for Regan's Introduction (which surveys metaethical and normative theory), each article ends with a helpful discussion of suggested reading. All the articles are excellent and readable. Articles include: Dale Jamieson, "The City Around Us"; Tibor R. Machan, "Pollution and Political Theory"; K. S. Schrader-Frechette, "Ethics and Energy"; Mark Sagoff, "Ethics and Environmental Law"; Robert L. Simon, "Troubled Waters: Global Justice and Ocean Resources"; Annette Baier, "For the Sake of Future Generations"; Alastair S. Gunn, "Preserving Rare Species"; and Edward Johnson, "Treating the Dirt."

Rolston, Holmes, III, *Environmental Ethics.* Philadelphia: Temple University Press, 1988.

A systematic account of values carried by the natural world, coupled with an inquiry into duties toward animals, plants, species, and ecosystems. A comprehensive philosophy of nature is illustrated by and integrated with numerous actual examples of ethical decisions made in encounters with fauna and flora – bighorn sheep, whales, ducks, butterflies, sequoias – and with endangered species and threatened ecosystems. The ethics developed is informed throughout by ecological science and evolutionary biology, with attention to the logic of moving from what *is* in nature to what *ought* to be. The ethical theory is applied in detail to social, public, and business policy. The ethics concludes by exploring the historical experiences of personal residence in a surrounding environment – what it means to live as responsible human beings in the community of life on Earth.

Rolston, Holmes, III, *Philosophy Gone Wild.* Buffalo: Prometheus Books,1986. 269 pp. Index.

This is a collection of fifteen essays previously published (1968-85) in diverse publications, such as *Ethics, BioScience, Environmental Ethics, Inquiry, Natural History,* and *Virginia Wildlife*. The articles can be read individually or in topically related groups. Rolston argues that nature has nonanthropocentric intrinsic and holistic value. Denying the is/ought fallacy, he maintains that values are natural in the sense that they objectively emerge out of ecosystems. Human values carried by nature are a product of the interrelationship of human persons with an objective environment. Parts I and II are metaethical and normative, concerning ethics and values. Part III focuses on three specific practical issues: economics, wildlands, and endangered species. Finally, Part IV is an inspirational account of experiences in nature – aesthetic, serene, mysterious, awesome.

Sagoff, Mark, *The Economy of the Earth: Philosophy, Law, and the Environment*. New York: Cambridge University Press, 1988.

Scherer, Donald, and Thomas Attig, eds., *Ethics and the Environment.* Englewood Cliffs, NJ: Prentice-Hall, 1983. 236 pp. Bibliography. No index.

Twenty articles are in this anthology. Nine concern establishing a theoretical basis for an environmental ethic (Leopold [two essays], Murdy, Sagoff, Goodpaster, Rolston, Callicott, Scherer, and Rodman); three concern land use (Hargrove, Soper, and Chief Justice Hallows); four concern cost-benefit analysis (MacIntyre, Socolow, Gewirth, and Potter); and four concern individual vs. collective choices (Blackstone, Scherer, Schelling, and Sagoff). The book is intended as a text for courses on contemporary moral problems or environmental ethics.

Singer, Peter, *Animal Liberation*. New York: Avon Books, 1975. 297 pp. Appendixes. Index. Paper.

Although Singer now endorses "preferential" utilitarianism, his argument in *Animal Liberation* is classical (hedonistic) utilitarianism and the position for which he is best known. Singer exposes the abuses of high-technology, "factory" agriculture and concludes that vegetarianism is morally obligatory to help stop the abuses. The book is considered to be the "Bible" of the animal liberation movement. Chapters are included on animal research and "speciesism." Very readable.

Stone, Christopher F., *Earth and Other Ethics*. New York: Harper and Row, 1987.

Taylor, Paul, *Respect for Nature*. Princeton: Princeton University Press, 1986. 329 pp. Index. Bibliography.

Taylor locates value in entities that are teleological centers of life—in entities having a good of their own that can be furthered or damaged by moral agents. So, for example, rocks are excluded but plants are included. Normatively, no species is superior, because all are teleological centers of life. Probably challenging for most undergraduates. A vigorous biocentrism, denying anthropocentrism.

Van DeVeer, Donald, and Christian Pierce, eds., *People, Penguins, and Plastic Trees: Basic Issues in Environmental Ethics.* Belmont, California: Wadsworth, 1986. 268 pp. Bibliography. List of organizations. Paper.

This anthology includes twenty-five articles in seven sections, and each section is introduced with brief summaries of the articles. The authors of the articles are generally leaders in their fields. Section topics are: animals as resources, land and trees, species preservation, wilderness, foundations for an environmental ethic, economics and marketability, and cost-benefit analysis. The articles are readable for undergraduates.

Wenz, Peter S., *Environmental Justice*. Albany: State University of New York Press., 1988.

Wilkinson, Loren, ed., *Earthkeeping: Christian Stewardship of Natural Resources.* Grand Rapids: Eerdmans, 1980.

Twenty-three

Futurism

Allen R. Utke

Overview of Unit Topic

It is our human ability to reach mentally beyond ourselves in an ever-widening and even timeless quest for knowledge, understanding and purpose that essentially sets us apart from the other forms of life on the earth. In one major facet of that mental outreach, humans have apparently always had an incurable desire, need and even compulsion to know, understand and foresee the future. The motivation behind that question would seem to lie in the fact that the seemingly ageless, apparently innate, ultimate questions of life not only include Who am I? and Why am I here? but also What should I be doing? and Where am I going?

Those throughout history who have had a greater than average desire, need, and even compulsion to understand, foresee, and mold the future, for whatever their reason(s) (e.g. curiosity, fear, personal gain, desire to improve the human condition, etc.) could inclusively be called "futurists" today. The methodology of such "futurists," whatever it might be, could thus also inclusively be called "futurism." It should be pointed out, however, that before the terms "futurist" and "futurism" were coined in the late 20th century, other terms were previously in use.

Actually, there have been four, quite different, specific types or classes of futurists and futurism in history. The first and oldest type, of unknown origins, has more traditionally been termed magic (reading crystal balls, palms, tarot cards, the entrails of sheep, etc.) and prophecy. The second type dates back to Plato and has more traditionally been termed utopianism. The third type, which largely originated in the late 1800's, has traditionally been termed science fiction. The fourth and most recent type of futurism has only appeared within the last generation or so, and might be termed twentieth century futurism.

Twentieth century futurism emerged in history after World War II, when after a half-century of increasing historical complexity, flux, and "future shock," various individuals, primarily in the military, began to see clearly that humankind could no longer afford simply to "drift into the future." Several military projects were then initiated that were designed to forecast the future directly in terms of weaponry and warfare. The spin-off of various individuals and methodologies from those efforts subsequently led to the establishment of such futuristic "think tanks" as RAND, the Hudson Institute, the Brookings Institute, etc.

In 1964, Bertrand de Jouvenel, a noted French economist and philosopher, wrote a book titled *The Art of Conjecture*, in which he 1) laid out the philosophical groundwork for developing futurism as a major new 20th century human endeavor 2) collected and summarized the new methodologies then available and 3) called for the widespread societal application of futurism. De Jouvenel has subsequently been termed "the father of futurism," and *The Art of Conjecture* has been labelled "a classic" of futurist literature.

The growth of futurism has been extremely impressive since 1964. Much of that growth has been centered in and around the World Future Society and its journal, *The Futurist*, both of which were established in the mid-1960's. The World Future Society currently has chapters in over 200 cities in the world, has over 35,000 members worldwide, and holds a global conference very four years that attracts over 5,000 participants from around the world.

Twentieth century futurism currently has over 40 distinct, technical, mathematical, scientific, historically new methods available for futures forecasting and prognostication. Each of the methods falls into one of three general classes. Exploratory methods (e.g. trend and S-curves, precursors, causal models, cross-matrix indexes, scenarios, etc.) generally operate by extrapolating the known past and present into an unknown future. In normative methods (e.g. morphological diagrams, relevance trees, mission flaw diagrams, etc.) one decides upon a desired future and then attempts to determine how to reach it. Various "miscellaneous" techniques (e.g. Delphi analysis, computer simulations, technological assessment, systems analysis, etc.) combine both exploratory and normative features.

The appeal and power of twentieth century futurism lies in its flexibility and scope. Its methodology can be applied to the disciplinary and/or interdisciplinary, simple, intermediate, or complex prognostication of "anything." For example, one can forecast the future price of a project, or the future of the world, using the same technique(s). Of course the more complex the question or problem to be studied, the less agreement one might expect among various futurists as to specifically what methodology should be used. Thus the more complex, the more controversial the result of such a study can be expected to be. A "true" futurist will therefore acknowledge, especially in the case of very complex questions and problems, that his or her forecast must be placed within the context of a range of possible alternative futures. Such an admission does not preclude a futurist from emphasizing his or her own favored and/or desired alternative future, but he or she should always be careful to label it as such.

Attempting to forecast the future of the world (global prognostication) is the most complex problem that a futurist might tackle. The problem is also inherently complicated from within by the fact that most futurists operate under an open parameter in global prognostication wherein they view the future of the world as being open, flexible, and thus moldable by human beings. [Note: The author has developed his own methodology for global prognostication, which he calls Level Five Prognostication. The methodology can not only be used to forecast global alternative futures, but also to classify and evaluate the efforts of other futurists in this area.]

Most futurists who have attempted global prognostication agree that, at a minimum, the world now faces both serious foreseeable and extensively unforeseeable problems that, at best, are going to be difficult to solve. The foreseeable problems largely originate in the 20th century exponential growth of population, urbanization, industrialization, resource and energy consumption, demand for food, and generation of pollution. The unforeseeable problems largely originate in the complexity, flux, and "future shock" being produced by the exponential growth of knowledge, information and technology, exponential growth which has in turn produced the other seven types of exponential growth mentioned previously. [Note: The author contends that because of all of the aforementioned exponential growth, we now live in the most abnormal, unpredictable, and dangerous age in history, an age where, for the first time in history, we now face the possibility of global historical terminality.]

In terms of possible solutions to such global problems, most futurists believe that humankind now finds itself in an age of great historical opportunity as well as danger. They believe that we are currently in the early stages of a major historical epochal shift in which we are now beginning to move away from our modern industrial age, toward a new post-industrial and post-modern age. We thus still largely have the opportunity to select and attempt to establish the alternative future of our choice. If our goal is to build a sustainable, participatory and just post-modern society, however, most futurists believe that we first need to initiate a societal physical revolution in the way we currently reductionistically act and operate in nature. That revolution will have to be centered on the eventual stabilization of global population and industrialization, although various futurists disagree as to the specific definition of the word "eventual."

Most futurists also agree that a prerequisite paradigmatic shift or mental revolution will be needed to initiate the needed physical revolution. However, they disagree as to how to initiate such a societal paradigm shift, and upon what specific paradigmatic traits it should be based. [Note: The author contends that a scientifically reformulated argument from design, natural theology and philosophy of nature could be key elements in the new needed physical and mental revolutions that in turn are keys to establishing a now much needed post-industrial and post-modern age.]

Importance and Utility of Unit Topic

Futurists contend that teaching of any kind, and on any level, must now incorporate a greater emphasis on the future. In this regard, they also advocate the further incorporation of a unit on futurism into existing courses whenever possible, and even the development of full courses on futurism, if possible [Note: The author's course, open to any student, is titled "Exploring The Future: An Introduction to Futurism.] Of course, the futurist's ultimate goal is to produce an alternative future that will save the future. In that regard, it should be obvious that futurists are extremely interested in the changing concepts of nature and God that are now beginning to appear on the frontiers of intellectual thought. For they are beginning to view such changes in thought as possibly playing increasingly important roles in the needed societal paradigmatic and physical shifts and revolutions for which they are now calling.

As one becomes more deeply involved in futurism, one begins to "feel" the historical immediacy of what one is doing, and begins to "see" the need to carry the banner of futurism beyond the classroom. In that regard, futurists invite all interested persons, of whatever background and expertise, to use futurism as an international, interdisciplinary outlet and forum to test and broadly disseminate their knowledge relative to the future, both within futurism itself, and/or beyond, to the public at large. Of course, such efforts necessitate expressing one's knowledge in a way that is accessible to a wider range of persons than just one's students and disciplinary, scholarly peers. In other words, the more one begins to "feel" the importance of futurism, the more one begins to "feel" the need to pick up the banner of futurism and carry it into the world whenever one can. That banner simply says, "The Future is Now!"

Keyed Annotated Bibliography for Unit

It should be pointed out that although futurism has its own vocabulary, terminology, and language, it is an interdisciplinary vocabulary, terminology, and language that is readily understandable by anyone of reasonable intelligence. All of the following references should thus be readable and understandable by educators, and most students and lay persons. When combined with the previous discussion, the references should provide an introductory understanding of the subject of futurism sufficient to begin to inject that understanding into the classroom and/or beyond. In this regard, the author would like to extend an offer to attempt to help anyone in such endeavors, in any way he can.

A. *The Origins of Twentieth Century Futurism*

The Art of Conjecture, by Bertrand de Jouvenel, Basic Books, New York, 1967. See previous discussion on page 242.

B. *The History, Terminology, Methodology and Resources of Twentieth Century Futurism*

The Study of the Future: An Introduction to the Art and Science of Understanding and Shaping Tomorrow's World, by Edward Cornish, The World Future society, Washington, D.C., 1977.

A general introduction to futurism and future studies. Various chapters discuss the history of the futurist movement, ways to introduce future-oriented thinking into organizations, the philosophical assumptions underlying studies of the future, methods of forecasting, current thinking about what may happen as a result of the current revolutionary changes in human society, etc. The volume also includes detailed descriptions of the life and thinking of certain prominent futurists and an annotated guide to further reading. An excellent text for an introductory course on futurism or a unit on futurism in an existing course.

The Future: A Guide to Information Sources, World Future Society, Washington, D.C., updated yearly.

A directory of organizations, individuals, books, educational programs, films, and other resources in futurism, and a glossary of terms used in futurism.

The World Future Society, 4916 St. Elmo Avenue, Washington, DC, 20014.

The central focus for those wishing to "plug in" to futurism (e.g. purchase books and other materials, attend meetings, present papers, publish articles, etc.). The official journal of the World Future Society is *The Futurist*, which is published bi-monthly. Current membership in the World Future Society is $25 per year, which includes a subscription to *The Futurist*.

Worldwatch Institute, 1776 Massachusetts Avenue NW, Washington, D.C.

An excellent source of data and information relative to futurism. The Worldwatch Institute, under the directorship of Lester R. Brown, publishes a yearly volume titled *The State of the World,* and several in-depth "Worldwatch Papers" each year on various, specific aspects of current global problems. A membership fee of $41 per year brings one all of the Institute's publications each year.

C. *Global Prognostication and Its Recent Findings and Conclusions*

"Level Five Prognostication," by Allen R. Utke, in *Applied Systems and Cybernetics*, edited by G. E. Lasker, Volume 1, *The Quality of Life: Systems Approaches*, Pergamon Press, New York, 1981, pp. 494-500.

See previous discussion on page 244.

The Limits to Growth, by Dennis Meadows *et al.*, Universe Books, New York, 1972.

The report prepared by Dennis Meadows *et al.* on the Club of Rome study of world trends. The researchers used the computerized systems-dynamics technique developed by

Jay Forrester in the late 1960's at MIT. The report argues that if present patterns of rapid population and capital growth are allowed to continue, the world faces a "disastrous collapse." It could be argued that the concept of global "limits to growth" could be the most important new idea to appear in the 20th century.

The Global 2000 Report to the President, Superintendent of Documents, U.S. Government Printing Office, Washington, D.C. 20402.

A report in three volumes (Summary, stock no. 041-011-0037-8, $5; Technical, stock no. 041-011-00038-6, $14; Documentation, stock no. 041-011-00051-3, $9.50) summarizing the forecast of the world in the year 2000 which former president Jimmy Carter commissioned while in office in 1977. Generally pessimistic about the world in the 21st century, unless various countermeasures are soon put in motion to counter current trends, the report is the first and (to date) only extensive global prognostication that the U.S. government has attempted.

The Resourceful Earth: A Response to Global 2000, by Herman Kahn, Oxford Press, New York, 1984.

Under the heading of "alternative futures," the dean of optimistic futurists replies to the "doom-saying" conclusions of the *Limits to Growth* and *The Global 2000 Report to the President*.

D. *Toward A Post-Modern Age: The Need for a Paradigm Shift in Society*

Future Shock, by Alvin Toffler, Random House, New York, 1970.

The best-seller that has sold over six million copies and been translated into 20 different languages. Toffler argues that increasing numbers of people are suffering from the impact of rapid social change. He also argues that the problem will get worse before it gets better. A final chapter proposes a number of ways in which this society can learn to cope with future shock.

The Turning Point: Science, Society, and the Rising Culture, by F. Capra, Simon and Schuster, New York, 1982.

The world is approaching a turning point, says physicist Capra. A massive shift in the perception of reality is underway, with thinkers in many disciplines beginning to move away from the traditional reductionist, mechanical world view to an ecological, holistic systems paradigm. An excellent summary of where the relationship of science, philosophy, and futurism stands today.

Critical Path, by Buckminster Fuller, St. Martin's Press, New York, 1981.

A book much like Capra's above but with an added emphasis on the value of theology, the God concept, and "design" in the universe in considerations of where the world is headed.

E. *Futurism and Education*

Education and the Future: Selected Articles on Education from The Futurist: A journal of Forecasts, Trends, and Ideas about the Future and the World Future Society, a bulletin of the World Future Society, 1980.

Teaching the Future: A Guide to Future-Orientated Education, by Draper L. Kauffman, ETC Publications, Palm Springs, California, 1976.

A practical handbook for classroom teachers interested in future-oriented education, with an emphasis on teaching methods and resources which have proven effective and flexible. The book contains many exercises on ways of thinking about the future, applicable to a wide range of educational levels and classroom settings. It also has a scenario for role-playing and a guide to literature, films, and simulation games.

Futurism and Future Studies, by Draper L. Kauffman, National Education Association, Washington, DC 1980.

A continuation and elaboration of the reference above.

Introducing the Participants & Faculty

Walter W. Artus is Professor of Philosophy and has taught at St. John's University, Jamaica, New York, since 1959. His main areas of interest are metaphysics, medieval philosophy, early Franciscan thinkers, and Ramon Llull. He is the author of numerous articles on Llull.

David K. Clark is now Associate Professor of Theology at Bethel Theological Seminary, St. Paul, Minnesota, though while participating at the Institute was Associate Professor of Philosophy and Theology at Toccoa Falls College, Toccoa, Georgia. His newest project is the book, *Apologetics in the New Age*, due for publication in 1989.

Bowman L. Clarke is Professor of Philosophy and Acting Head of the Department of Philosophy at the University of Georgia, where he has taught since 1961. He is author of *Language and Natural Theology* (1966) and co-editor of *God and Temporality* (1984), as well as many articles in philosophy of religion, metaphysics, and logic. His research interests combine pursuit of advanced logic with Whitehead's metaphysics. He is editor of the *International Journal for Philosophy of Religion*.

J. A. Colombo is Assistant Professor in the Department of Theological and Religious Studies at the University of San Diego, where he teaches fundamental and systematic theology.

Donald A. Crosby is Professor of Philosophy at Colorado State University. He is author of *Horace Bushnell's Theory of Language:*

In the Context of Other Nineteenth-Century Philosophers of Language (1975) and *Interpretive Theories of Religion* (1981). His latest book is *The Specter of the Absurd: Sources and Criticism of Modern Nihilism* (1988). His research interests are in process metaphysics, philosophy of nature, and philosophy of religion.

Ralph Ellis is Associate Professor of Philosophy at Clark College, Atlanta, Georgia. He has recently published a book, *An Ontology of Consciousness*, and has written a number of articles on the philosophy of mind and of the social sciences, phenomenology, ethics, policy analysis, causal theory, and the philosophy of science. In addition to his philosophical education, he holds a post-doctoral graduate degree in Public Affairs. He is currently writing a book on the epistemology of ethical theory.

Frederick Ferré is Research Professor of Philosophy at the University of Georgia. He is author of *Language, Logic and God* (1962), *Basic Modern Philosophy of Religion* (1967), and *Shaping the Future* (1976), and is editor of William Paley's *Natural Theology* and August Comte's *Introduction to the Positive Philosophy*. His most recent book is *Philosophy of Technology* (1988), and he combines interests in philosophy of religion and ethics with philosophy of technology and environment. He is editor of *Research in Philosophy and Technology*.

William J. Garland is Professor and Chair of the Department of Philosophy at the University of the South, Sewanee, Tennessee. He has published articles on process philosophy and continues research into Whitehead's metaphysics and theory of value as well as into the metaphysical justification of ecological concerns.

Walter Gulick is Professor of Philosophy, Humanities, and Religious Studies at Eastern Montana College, Billings, Montana. He has published articles on a broad range of topics, many of which bear on the interpretation of lived meaning. Typical titles of his articles include: "Archetypal Experiences," "Linking Head, Heart, and Habitat: The Role of Myths," "Michael Polanyi's Theory of Meaning and Reality," and "Reconnecting Geertz's Middle World."

John L. Hammond is Professor of Philosophy at Portland State University, Portland, Oregon. His research interests are philosophy of ecology, ethics, philosophy of religion, and relativity theory. Titles of his articles include: "Relativity and Relativism," "Wilderness and Heritage Values," and "Theism and the Moral Point of View."

Frank R. Harrison, III, is Professor of Philosophy at the University of Georgia, where he has taught since 1962. He combines interests in ancient and medieval philosophy with current developments in philosophy of language, computer intelligence, and philosophy of mind. Author of several dozen scholarly articles, his recent work includes "Language, Knowledge, and God." He is currently putting the finishing touches on a new book in logic.

Stanley M. Harrison is Associate Professor Philosophy at Marquette University, Milwaukee, Wisconsin. His special interests include classical American philosophy, process philosophy, philosophy of religion, and philosophy of human person (with a focus on the importance of developments in biology and related disciplines for rethinking traditional issues about human nature). He co-edited *The Life of Religion* (1986) and recently published an article entitled "Walker Percy's Unspeakable Self."

Wesley L. Henry is Assistant Professor of Philosophy and Honors Director at Tennessee Technological University, Cookeville, Tennessee. In connection with his doctoral work at Vanderbilt University, he wrote a dissertation on 18th century natural theologies. His research interests presently include topics in philosophy of religion and environmental ethics.

John P. Hittinger is Associate Professor and Chair in the Department of Philosophy and Religious Studies at the College of St. Francis, Joliet, Illinois. He wrote his doctoral dissertation at Catholic University on John Locke's ethics. He has published articles in areas of political philosophy and metaphysics and is presently working on topics in St. Augustine's philosophy of religion. He is editing a book on 20th century Catholic philosophers.

Donald Petar Jarnevic is Associate Professor of Philosophy at Mercy College of Detroit, Michigan. His major research interests are in philosophy of religion and medieval philosophy.

Fr. Justin Nolan, O.S.B., is Associate Professor of Philosophy at St. Vincent College, Latrobe, Pennsylvania. His current research interest draws him to questions in the philosophy of nature.

Don H. Olive is Professor and Coordinator of the Department of Philosophy in Carson-Newman College, Jefferson City, Tennessee. Principal areas of interest are philosophy of religion and philosophical theology. His publications include *Wolfhart Pannenberg: Maker of the Modern Theological Mind; A Word about Words; Practical Reasoning: A Handbook for Beginners;* and *Introduction to Logic and Scientific Method.*

Stanley Riukas is Professor of Philosophy at West Chester University, West Chester, Pennsylvania. He is the author of *God: Myth, Symbol, and Reality; A Study of C. G. Jung's Psychology* (1967) and an article, "A Critical Examination of the Metaphysical Foundations of Transcendental Meditation." His main research interests are in philosophy of mind, Hegel's philosophy of religion and of science, and Spinoza's metaphysics.

Holmes Rolston, III, is Professor of Philosophy at Colorado State University. He is author of the books: *Science and Religion: A*

Critical Survey; Philosophy Gone Wild; Environmental Ethics; and *Religious Inquiry – Participation and Detachment.*

James F. Salmon, S.J., is currently Treasurer of the Maryland Province of the Jesuit Order. With a Ph.D. in chemistry from the University of Pennsylvania, he has taught chemistry at Loyola College of Maryland, the Johns Hopkins University, and Wheeling Jesuit College. He has also been a member of the theology departments of Loyola, Wheeling, and Georgetown University. Besides co-authoring five research papers and three books in advanced chemistry, he is co-editor of *Teilhard and the Unity of Knowledge* and author of the monograph, *Teilhard and Prigogine.*

Walter Thomas Schmid teaches philosophy at the University of North Carolina at Wilmington. He studied Plato with Robert Brumbaugh, Hans-Georg Gadamer, and Gregory Vlastos. He has published several articles on the Socratic dialogues, including "The Socratic Conception of Courage" and "Socratic Moderation and Self-Knowledge," and is currently working on the relationship between justice and the other virtues.

Karl Schmitz-Moormann is Professor of Philosophy and Theology at the Fachhochschule, Dortmund, West Germany. He has published many articles on the views of Teilhard de Chardin and has been a leading figure behind both the first and second European Conferences on Science and Religion.

Edward L. Schoen is Professor of Philosophy at Western Kentucky University, Bowling Green, Kentucky. His *Religious Explanations: A Model from the Sciences* (1985), was devoted to exploring parallels between explanatory strategies used in the sciences and those founds in religious contexts. More recently, he has been investigating the epistemic value of religious experience in light of the evidential roles played by perception in the sciences. Currently, he is carrying these research interests into the classroom in a new introductory course entitled "Religion and Modern Science."

David Schrader is Associate Professor of Philosophy and Chair of the Department of Religion and Philosophy at Austin College in Sherman, Texas. He is the editor of *Ethics and the Practice of Law* (1988) and the author of a number of articles in philosophy of religion and ethics. His current research is centered around the intersection of ethics with economic theory.

Robert C. Smith is an Associate Professor of Philosophy and Religion at Trenton State College, Trenton, New Jersey. Recently he has been a Visiting Lecturer at the C. G. Jung Institute in Küsnacht, Switzerland. As a Danforth Associate he has directed conferences concerned with values in higher education. A Coolidge Fellow, he is the editor of *Pagan and Christian Anxiety,* an analysis of the ideas of late antiquity. He is currently working on a manuscript on Jung and creativity.

Stanley T. Sutphin is Professor and Chairperson, Department of Philosophy, Elizabethtown College, Elizabethtown, Pennsylvania. He has taught at his present post for twenty-five years. He is author of *Options in Contemporary Theology* (1987, revised). His current research interest is in characteristics of the mind and brain.

Dennis Temple is Professor and Chair of the Department of Philosophy at Roosevelt University, Chicago, Illinois. He has presented papers at meetings of the American Philosophical Association and the World Congress of Philosophy. He has published articles in *American Philosophical Quarterly, Philosophy of Science,* and elsewhere, and is currently at work on a book reassessing the argument from design in the light of current views of scientific method.

Allen R. Utke is Professor of Chemistry at the University of Wisconsin, Oshkosh, Wisconsin. He is intensely engaged in future studies and currently on extended leave in Malaysia.

Jack Weir is Professor and Chair of the Philosophy Department at Hardin-Simmons University in Abilene, Texas. Although a generalist in his teaching, his research specializes in ethics and philosophy of religion. His recent publications on animal ethics and environmental ethics have appeared in *Contemporary Philosophy* and *Southwest Philosophical Studies*. Currently he is working on a book on animal ethics and is co-editor of *Southwest Philosophical Studies*.